WHO IS THE REAL JESUS?

ANSWERS TO 25 OF THE TOUGHEST QUESTIONS ABOUT THE REAL JESUS

Simple & Straight-Forward to the Point Answers
that will Change Your Life!

BY DR. RUTH TANYI

Who is the Real Jesus? Answers to 25 of the Toughest Questions About the Real Jesus. Simple & Straight-Forward to the Point Answers that will Change Your Life!

Copyright © 2018 by Dr Ruth Tanyi.
Published by   Dr Ruth Tanyi Ministries, Inc
                 P O BOX 1806
                 Loma Linda, CA, 92354, USA.
                 www.DrRuthtanyi.org

Cover design and Interior layout by: AJ Design

Additional copies of this book can be obtained from:
                 Online: www.DrRuthtanyi.org
                 Email: Info@DrRuthtanyi.org

We want to hear from you. Please send your comments and/or testimonies about this book to: Info@DrRuthTanyi.org or write to:

        Dr. Ruth Tanyi Ministries, Inc
        P O BOX 1806
        Loma Linda, CA, 92354, USA.

If you find any error in the citation of Scripture anywhere in this book, kindly contact us so we can make the necessary corrections, thank you.

ISBN 9780998668932
Library of Congress Control Number: 2018903799

CONTENTS

INTRODUCTION

Today, many individuals, including Protestants, Roman Catholics, Orthodox Christians, and even the pseudo Christian Religious cults such as the Jehovah's Witnesses and the Mormons all call upon the name of Jesus Christ. But which Jesus is it? Is it the Jesus of the Christian Bible or another?

Friend, do not be deceived, there is Only One Jesus, the Jesus Christ of the true Christian Bible, although many people want Him to fit into their definition, rather than accepting Him as He has revealed Himself to us. Many individuals outright reject the true identity of the Lord Jesus, and instead, refer to Him as just "a teacher," "a prophet", "a perfect man", or just "a good moral person", but Jesus Christ was beyond all of these titles!

Others questioned and are still questioning whether or not He actually existed in time and space on this earth. For those of you struggling with understanding the real identity of Jesus Christ, **this book provides biblically-based, simple and straight forward, to the point answers to 25 of the toughest questions about the "real" Jesus Christ of the True Christian Bible.** These answers will definitely provide much clarity and enhance your understanding of who Jesus Christ is. Although I could have elaborated on each of the answers provided in this book, I decided to keep them simple and "to the point," for simplicity.

To the true Christian, it is my hope that this book will draw you closer to the Lord Jesus as your personal friend, and offer you a simple tool to assist you to defend your faith. If you do not yet have a personal relationship with God through His Only Son Jesus Christ, it is my prayer that this book will provide you with some basic answers you have been searching for, and hopefully, enable you to open your heart and allow God to reveal His Only Son, Jesus Christ, to you, as your personal Lord and Savior.

Upon studying and meditating on the answers provided in this book, you will, at last, come to the firm conclusion that there is Only One Jesus Christ as revealed in the Christian Bible. And as you open your heart and allow the Holy Spirit to reveal Christ to you, I pray that you will be well positioned to easily discern His unfathomable love for you.

February, 2018

DEDICATION

To you the reader, who is being drawn by the Holy Spirit to want to know the "real" Jesus Christ of the True Christian Bible. I believe that this book will answer many of your questions, and hopefully, do one of two things: (1) provide clarity about the true identity of our Lord Jesus Christ, thereby enabling you to be willing to become His true follower; or (2) encourage you, if you are already a true Christian, to rededicate your life to the Lord and be fully (100%) focused on Him, as your Lord and Savior, and as your personal friend. I pray for the Holy Spirit to reveal Christ to you personally, that way you will be grounded in your true identity in Him!

OTHER TEACHING MATERIALS BY DR TANYI TO HELP YOU GROW WITH GOD THROUGH CHRIST

BOOKS BY DR TANYI:

- *Are You Moving Forward with Jesus? | How to Excel In Your Identity in Christ.*
- *Answers to 25 of the Toughest Questions About the Real Jesus.*
- *Can I trust the Bible as God's Word? How do I Know? What Is the Evidence?*
- *Faith to Receive God's Promises. How to "Walk" in Biblical Faith and Allow the Blessings of God to Chase You.*

COMING SOON!

- *13 Reasons Why People Get Sick! A Biblical Perspective & Remedies.*
- *Did God Really Say that? How to Overcome Doubt and Receive God's Promises: 10 Life-Changing Lessons Learned from Overcoming Metastasis Colon Cancer.*
- *A True Story of God's Unconditional Grace and Love: Healed by the Stripes of Jesus: My Story! My Miracle! How I Overcame Metastasis Colon Cancer.*

AUDIO CD TEACHING LIBRARY:

- *The Heart of True Christianity: The Gospel Message of Jesus Christ: Answers to 10 Major Questions Pertaining to Your Salvation in Christ Jesus.*
- *What Are the Gifts of the Spirit?*
- *Holy Spirit-Led Healthy Emotions: The Fruit of the Spirit and Your Health.*
- *How to Overcome Doubt and Receive God's Promises.*
- *13 Reasons Why People Get Sick: A Biblical Perspective & Remedies.*
- *Unforgiveness and Other Toxic Emotions: How to Walk in Forgiveness.*
- *Live Above Your Fears & Overcome Sicknesses and Diseases.*
- *Be Anxious No More.*
- *Daily Habits For Your Soul.*
- *Faith to Receive God's Promises | How to "Walk" in Biblical Faith and Allow the Blessings of God to Chase You.*

- *Are You Moving Forward with Jesus? | How to Excel In Your Identity in Christ.*

Grow in the Word of God and Receive His blessings through our Discipleship Bible Teaching Series.

The **Audio Podcast Series**, titled *"Biblical Principles for a Blessed Life,"* is an in-depth teaching through the entire Bible, from Genesis to the book of Revelation, focusing on major biblical principles, and teaching you how to apply those principles daily and receive God's blessings.

Biblical Preventive Health with Dr Ruth®

Biblical Preventive Health with Dr Ruth® is an educational magazine, which will educate individuals on how to integrate Bible-based principles into their lives, thereby preventing and overcoming sicknesses and diseases. You have heard what Medicine has to say! But do you know what the Bible says about a host of diseases plaguing people today? This magazine will teach you how to view your health from a godly perspective, and it offers practical recommendations to take care of God's temple.

13 Reasons Why True Christianity is Different: A Wall Mount Poster

This wall mount poster answers the question many individuals often ask: What makes Christianity different? This evangelistic poster will remind you daily of your unique relationship with God through Christ, and provide answers to confidently educate others and defend your faith. You will never be dumbfounded when asked to explain why your faith in Christ is unique, compared to other religions.

Obtaining Ministry Resources

To obtain additional copies of this book, or to get more information about the above ministry resources, please visit our Website:

www.DrRuthTanyi.org. You can also email, write or call us:

Dr. Ruth Tanyi Ministries, Inc
P O BOX 1806 | Loma Linda, CA, 92354, USA.
Email: Info@DrRuthtanyi.org
Phone: (909) 383-7978

....

WHO REALLY IS JESUS CHRIST?

Question # 1: Who Really Is Jesus Christ?

Answer: Jesus Christ had two distinct natures: Deity (i.e., He was God 100%) and a human being (100%), like one of us.

Jesus Christ is the most significant individual who has ever existed in the history of the world. He was the Only Son of God. He was fully God, and fully man. Although the name, "Jesus," was a very popular name among the Jews during the time the Lord Jesus lived on this earth, there is Only One True Jesus Christ.   And the name "Christ" means the "Messiah", meaning, the One anointed (i.e., set apart and endued with supernatural abilities) by God as the Savior of the world. Thus, Jesus Christ was the Messiah, God's gift to Mankind as The Only Savior of the world (i.e., the savior to redeem Mankind from our Sinful Nature and deliver us from the kingdom of darkness, belonging to Satan).   Besides being the Messiah, other offices of Jesus Christ include that of (1) a prophet; (2) a King; and (3) a High Priest. Let us take a brief look at each of these offices.

Jesus Christ: God 100% and Man 100%

This is <u>The</u> major mystery about the person Jesus Christ. He was not half God and half Man. He was not just a man who had God in Him, and He was not just a man who revealed God to us or expressed the image of God. Rather, He was 100% God in nature and 100% human being in nature —

He had two very distinct natures: 100% Divine and 100% Human, called the hypostatic union, in Christian theology. These two natures are not mixed together or combined together to make a God-man "new nature" as some critics have said —NO, these were two separate unique natures, but yet operated as a single unit in the person Jesus Christ.

This is quite a mystery, and we accept it by faith, because that is how it has been revealed to us in the Bible. Through divine incarnation (i.e., God supernaturally became a human being), Jesus Christ was, and is the Word of God that was made flesh (i.e., a human being with flesh and bones); and the Word of God is eternal, meaning, it has always existed, thus pointing to the eternal nature of Christ Jesus. Hence, Jesus Christ was God, before He became a human being like one of us!

**By becoming a human being, the divine nature
of Jesus Christ was not inferior to God the
Father, nor did it change. Rather, the Word was
supernaturally joined with humanity as one (John
1:1-14; Colossians 2:9; Hebrews 1:3).**

The divine Son of God, Christ Jesus, is the second person of the Godhead, usually referred to as the Trinity (to be discussed later in this book).

References of Jesus Christ as God in the Holy Scripture

In the Bible there are numerous references of Jesus Christ as God, which are all **attributes of The God of the true Christian Bible**. Below are some of these biblical references:

> ➤ The fullness of the Deity dwells on Him (Colossians 2:9);

> ➤ He was worshipped as God at His birth (Matthew 2:2);

> ➤ He was an exact (i.e., 100%) representation of God Himself in His bodily form and existed even before the creation of the world, and He was involved in the creation of the heavens and the earth (Colossians 1:15-19);

> ➤ He is The Only One Who gives eternal life (John 10:28);

➢ He is The Only One Who can forgive All sins (Mark 2:10; Hebrews 1:3);

➢ He knows All things (John 21:17);

➢ He accepted to be worshiped as God (John 9:38; 20:28);

➢ He was, and is called God (Hebrews 1:8; John 20:28);

➢ He was sinless (1 John 3:5; Hebrews 4:15; 2 Corinthians 5:21 ;1 Peter 2:22);

➢ Much more, the Lord Jesus called Himself God (John 14:9; John 8:48-59), teaching us that, He has always existed, and will always exist, etc, etc.

References of Jesus Christ as Man in the Holy Scripture

Also, several scriptures refer to Jesus Christ as a human being in the Bible. Here are just a few of them:

➢ He was tempted by Satan as a mere human being (Matthew 4:1);

➢ He prayed to God the Father (John chapter 17);

➢ He was referred to by others as human being with flesh and bones, that is to say, He was referred to as Man (John 19:5);

➢ He was called the Son of Man (John 9:35-38);

➢ He grew in wisdom and stature, and had favor with

God and His fellow human beings (Luke 2:52);

➤ He experienced hunger, fatigue, and pain like a mere human being (John 19:28-29; Mark 11:12-13);

➤ He called God His Father and worshipped Him (Luke 23:46; John chapter 17);

➤ He was filled with the Holy Spirit (Luke 4:1) and as such operated in All of the gifts of the Spirit (see 1 Corinthians 12: 1-11), and performed miracles as a man (see the Gospels);

➤ He died (i.e., He experienced physical death like a mere human being and was buried) (Romans 5:8; Mark 15: 33-47);

➤ He ascended into heaven in bodily form (Acts 1: 1-11), etc, etc.

In spite of being a human being like one of us, Jesus Christ expressed the highest level of humility towards God the Father. Under the inspiration of the Holy Spirit, the Apostle Paul explained the humility of Christ:

Who, though he was in the form of God, did not count equality with God a thing to be grasped, but emptied himself, by taking the form of a servant, being born in the likeness of men. And being found in human form, he humbled himself by becoming obedient to the point of death, even death on a cross. Therefore God has highly exalted him and bestowed on him the name that

*is above every name, so that at the name of Jesus every knee
should bow, in heaven and on earth and under the earth, and
every tongue confess that Jesus Christ is Lord, to the glory of
God the Father* (Philippians 2:6-11), (emphasis author's).

Jesus Christ came to the earth primarily to perform
the will of God the Father, as obviously stated in the above
Scripture. His humanity (i.e., His human nature) was 100%
submissive to the will of God the Father. He "walked" in
perfect obedience to God the Father, and humbled Himself unto
His death, because of His unfathomable love for Mankind.

Jesus Christ as a Prophet

A prophet or prophetess of God is any individual
who reveals the "heart" of God to others, and speaks or
communicates on behalf of God. During the Old Testament
era, God revealed His thoughts through the prophets, such
as the prophets Jeremiah, Elijah, Samuel, etc. Jesus Christ
fulfilled the role of a prophet as He revealed the will of God
the Father to us throughout His ministry, and He only spoke the
things which he heard from the Father (see the Gospels). In the
Gospel accounts, the Lord Jesus also referred to Himself as a
prophet (see Matthew 13:57; Luke 13:33).

**Keep in mind that this was just one of the offices
of Jesus Christ, but He was more than "just" a prophet.
I insist on this because this is where the Muslims get
confused, by referring to Jesus Christ as "just" a prophet,
similar to Muhammad, their prophet. This deception and**

line of thinking by the Muslims is absolutely wrong. Jesus Christ was also God 100% as already described above, and not "just" a prophet.

Jesus Christ as a Priest

During the Old Testament era, the High Priest was the one who entered into the most holy of holies in the tabernacle (i.e., a physical building where the Spirit of God dwelled among the Israelites during the Old Testament era) and made animal sacrifices for the sins of the community at large, including his own sins. This Priestly role during the Old Testament was a foreshadow (i.e., representation) of the "real thing" Jesus Christ , who made the ultimate sacrifice, by dying on the cross as a sacrificial lamb offering for the sins of the entire human race: past, present and future sins (see Hebrews chapters 7 through 10).

However, while Jesus died for the sins of the world, each individual has to, by faith, accept His ultimate sacrifice in order to have a relationship with the Only True living God of the heavens and the earth: The God of the Bible. Today, Jesus Christ continues to act as The High Priest, for His true followers, interceding to God the Father, on their behalf (Romans 8:34).

Jesus Christ as a King

A king is a person who has authority to rule and reign over individuals, including bringing judgment upon them. Jesus Christ is described in the Bible as The Ultimate King. The

Bible describes Jesus Christ as the King of the Jews. At His birth, the Magi called Him King, they said: *"Where is the one who has been born king of the Jews? We saw his star when it rose and have come to worship him"* (Matthew 2:1-2), (emphasis author's).

And during his interrogation right before His crucifixion, the Lord Jesus accepted the title of king. The Gospel of Matthew records that: *Meanwhile Jesus stood before the governor, and the governor asked him, "Are you the king of the Jews?" "You have said so," Jesus replied* (27:11), (emphasis author's).

Then in the book of Revelation (which is the Revelation of Jesus Christ), the Lord Jesus is clearly portrayed as the **King of Kings and Lord of Lords** (Revelation 19:16), and He will judge the entire world. Under the inspiration of the Holy Spirit, the Apostle John tells us: **"I saw heaven standing open and there before me was a white horse, whose rider is called Faithful and True. With justice he judges and wages war"** (Revelation 19:11), (emphasis author's).

Jesus Christ is God's gift to you. Accepting to have a relationship with Him is simply a heartfelt decision. If you believe in your heart that Jesus Christ was God Himself in the flesh, that He died for your sins and was raised from the dead after 3 days as prophesied in the Bible, then you will become His follower. If you truly believe that, and you are ready to make Jesus Christ your personal Lord and Savior, and you are willing to denounce all other false ways or gods, in order to accept the One true living God of the Bible, then simply ask Him, Jesus Christ, to come into your heart right now, and He will. If you need help doing this, say the simple prayer below.

Take note that it is not the prayer that will earn you a relationship with God through Christ. Rather, you must first believe in your heart in Jesus Christ as your Messiah, then you will confess or pray out loud what you believe. If you need help confessing what you already believe in your heart that Jesus Christ is your Lord and Savior, then say this simple prayer aloud, if you are genuine:

*"Dear God, thank you for sending Jesus to die for **All** of my sins. I acknowledge that I am a sinner who needs help. I receive your forgiveness right now. I believe you are my Messiah, who died for my sins and was raised from the dead on the third day. I believe in **All** of your claims and works! Lord Jesus, I ask you to come into my life, right now, and make me a new person. I denounce all false gods in my life. By faith, I believe you have accepted me. Thank you God, in Jesus name, AMEN!"*

If you said that prayer genuinely, based on the authority of God's Word, you are a true Christian — a follower of Jesus Christ, and God Himself, in the form of His Spirit is living on the inside of you, right now, and you have been sealed by the Holy Spirit (Ephesians 1:13). You are now a child of God. Welcome into God's Kingdom, the Kingdom of Light! Hallelujah!

....

WHY DID JESUS CHRIST BECOME "FLESH"

Question # 2: Why Did Jesus Christ Become "Flesh"?

Answer: To redeem us from the Sinful Nature we all have inherited from Adam and Eve, and because of God's unconditional and unfathomable love for His creation, human beings.

The Bible records in Genesis chapters 1 and 2 how God created a perfect universe. But we are told in Genesis chapter 3 how the first human beings created by God, Adam and Eve were deceived by Satan, and as such transgressed God's law (i.e., sin knowingly against God), in spite of God's specific instructions to them not to eat fruit from a particular tree in the middle of the Garden of Eden. Once Adam and Eve disobeyed God and this sin took place, sin and death entered into God's perfect universe, and the entire human race was contaminated with a disease called sin, and subsequently inherited a Sinful Nature (Romans 3:23; 5:12-21).

We all have inherited this disease called sin, because all of us came from one common ancestors: Adam and Eve, although we might look different outwardly. By definition, sin is any offense against God's perfect standards knowingly or unknowingly. Some examples of sin include, but are not limited to: denying to accept Jesus Christ as God's sacrifice for your personal sins; unforgiveness towards others; idolatry (i.e., allowing other things, such as money, human relationships, careers, your children, spouse, etc, to have precedence in your life instead of God); envy; all sorts of sexual immorality such as sex before marriage, adultery, homosexuality, lesbianism, etc; telling lies; pride; jealousy; giving false witness against someone else; gossip; not treating your fellow humans with care and love; abusing the name of God; disrespect for authority; etc, etc, etc, the list is endless, and I am sure you know in your heart when you sin against God.

After Adam and Eve committed that sin in the Garden of Eden as recorded in Genesis chapter 3, human beings (i.e., Adam and Eve) "fell from grace", and because God is just, sin had to be punished. Thus, God cursed the soil and the Serpent. The Serpent was in fact, Satan himself, who manifested to Adam and Eve in the form of a Serpent and deceived them; God also pronounced punishment upon the entire human race. Since then, all human beings born of a woman come into this world as sinners, regardless of gender, geographical location, etc, because at birth, we all inherit that Sinful Nature from Adam and Eve.

God created the first Mankind: Adam and Eve, as tripartite beings, consisting of a mind, body and a spirit.

Hence, as part of the punishment against Adam and Eve after they disobeyed God, man's spirit (i.e., all human beings born into this world) became darkened, and Mankind could no longer fellowship with God who is holy, because of sin. You do not have to commit any act of sin to be a sinner, just being born into this world by a woman qualifies you as a sinner; who needs a Savior to regenerate that darkened spirit inherited at birth, before you could fellowship with God. We now live in a "fallen world", and things are not "perfect". So, since that " fall from grace" and its subsequent sin and death, all kinds of ungodliness and unrighteousness abound, and have perverted God's perfect creation.

Jesus Christ Became a Human Being Because of His Unconditional Love For Us

The Bible teaches that: " *For God so loved the world that he gave his one and only Son, that whoever believes in him shall not perish but have eternal life*" (John 3:16). This Scripture: John 3:16, is the most popular Scripture from the Bible, and it is the most powerful, because of the absolute Truth it espouses about God's unconditional love towards Mankind. God is love (1 John 4:8), and in His love, He did not want us, His creation, human beings, to remain in that "fallen state" forever, and to be defeated, ruled and dominated by the evil one, Satan, who deceived Adam and Eve.

God desires a relationship with us, His creation, thus in His love quest to have this relationship, He chose to "do something" about our "fallen state." God is perfectly holy and righteous, with no deceit, lie or darkness in Him. Since God is sinless, He could not, and cannot, and will not fellowship with us, Mankind, in our "fallen state." Thus, He chose to supernaturally become a human being, in the person of Jesus Christ, in order to reveal His true nature to us, and to redeem us (i.e., buy us back) from our "fallen state", and from the hands of Satan and his kingdom, the Kingdom of darkness.

To redeem us therefore, God Himself became a human being, like one of us, through the supernatural conception of Mary, and she gave birth to the Messiah, the Savior of the world.

Through His death and resurrection, Jesus Christ has redeemed Mankind from that "fallen state", but each one of us has to accept His redemption, and choose to be saved (i.e., to be given a regenerated or "new" spirit and become a true Christian), in order to have a direct relationship with God.

Also, Jesus Christ had to become flesh and bones so He could perfectly relate to our condition as human beings. Thus, by becoming "flesh" (i.e., flesh and bones) or a human being like one of us, Jesus Christ, totally understands our pain, sufferings and struggles, because He experienced all of these emotions Himself — He is the Only One who knows us and understands our deepest desires and troubles perfectly! We, as Christians, can trust that Jesus Christ, our Messiah, intimately understands all of our problems as human beings.

So, whatever you are experiencing today, be certain that Jesus Christ understands 100%, you can trust Him with your soul! No other human being in the history of the world can claim to know us perfectly, except Jesus Christ! If you do not know Him personally, I recommend that you ask Him into your life today, right now! You will not regret this decision! He is waiting for you to simply invite Him into your life right now! Tomorrow might be too late!

....

IS JESUS CHRIST REALLY
THE MESSIAH?

Question # 3: Is Jesus Christ Really the Messiah?

Answer: Yes, He is the Only human being who fulfilled **All** Old Testament Messianic prophecies 100%. He is, indeed, the Messiah!

You may be wondering why I am 100% certain about this answer. Due to space limitation in this book, I am unable to expound on this very relevant topic, which several text books have been written about. In brief, there are several reasons, but here are the three major reasons why we, as Christians, know beyond a shadow of doubt, that Jesus Christ was, and is, indeed the Messiah, the Savior of the world, Whose coming the Jews of the Old Testament era were looking forward to: (1) He fulfilled **All** of the Old Testament prophecies about the Messiah perfectly; (2) He performed miracles; (3) He was raised from the dead.

Besides the three major reasons noted above, other significant reasons include, but are not limited to (a) He revealed to us the true nature of God the Father (i.e., the Lord told His disciples that by knowing and seeing Him, they had seen God the Father, referring to His mannerisms such as love, compassion, hatred for evil, willingness to heal the sick, etc; (b) He authenticated the Holy Scriptures by quoting from it throughout His ministry, and pointed others to search the Scriptures about Himself, the Messiah, etc, (c) He forgave and still forgives sins, etc.

No other human being in the history of the world has ever, and will ever come close to performing the proven, and verifiable miracles that Jesus Christ performed. According to Vine's Dictionary of Old and New Testament Words, a miracle *is any "sign" "event", etc, which could not be produced by natural means, it has to come from God, who is supernatural.* As recorded in the Gospels, Jesus Christ performed all sorts of miracles, such as, but not limited to: (1) walking on water (see Mark 6:45-52); (2) raising the dead (see John 11:38-44; Mark 5:21-43); (3) healing the sick from physical, mental and emotional diseases (see Matthew 4: 23-25; see Matthew chapters 8 and 9); (4) calming the storm (see Matthew 8: 23-27); (5) obtaining money from the fish's mouth (e.g., Matthew 17:24-27); (6) feeding the multitudes (Mark 6:30-44); and (7) He Himself was raised from the dead, etc, which are all prophecies from the Old Testament of things that the Messiah would do.

According to Vine's Dictionary, a prophecy is defined as " *communicating forth the mind of God"; it is not just a "foretelling or a prediction."* A prophecy is a definite declaration of knowledge that cannot be known by mere natural means, it has to come from God. While many so called counterfeit Messiahs had surfaced even before the time of Jesus Christ, He is the Only One, in the history of the world, who undeniably fulfilled, exactly, all of the Old Testament Messianic prophecies.

There are hundreds of such prophecies in the Bible, but due to space limitation, I have only listed 9 on the table below. If you were to ask any unbiased statistician, he or she will agree that the chances of Jesus Christ being the Messiah, based on His fulfillment of Old Testament prophecies alone, is about 99.999% true, that is to say, essentially, 100%. With just 9 of those prophecies listed below, how can anyone deny that Christ Jesus was the Messiah? Only those who are biased would attempt to refute this fact, which in itself will be a futile effort, because numbers do not lie!

The interesting thing with numbers is that, they are "hard core facts" that no one can deny, although their interpretation can differ. Just by the notion of numbers being actual facts that cannot be refuted, how can any rational human being refute what even the statisticians are saying, that the numbers are pointing to the "hard core facts" that Jesus Christ, is indeed, the Messiah? Take a closer look at the table, and judge for yourself:

Jesus Christ and Bible Prophecies

OLD TESTAMENT PROPHECY	FULFILLED BY CHRIST JESUS
Isaiah 7:14	**Luke 1:26-33**
Prophecy: The birth of the Messiah.	**Fulfilled:**
Therefore the Lord himself will give you a sign: The virgin will conceive and give birth to a son, and will call him Immanuel.	*In the sixth month of Elizabeth's pregnancy, God sent the angel Gabriel to Nazareth, a town in Galilee, to a virgin pledged to be married to a man named Joseph, a descendant of David. The virgin's name was Mary. The angel went to her and said, "Greetings, you who are highly favored! The Lord is with you." Mary was greatly troubled at his words and wondered what kind of greeting this might be. But the angel said to her, "Do not be afraid, Mary; you have found favor with God. You will conceive and give birth to a son, and you are to call him Jesus..."*

OLD TESTAMENT PROPHECY	FULFILLED BY CHRIST JESUS
Isaiah 40:3-5	**Luke 3:3-6**
Prophecy: Forerunner of the Messiah (John the Baptist). *The voice of one crying in the wilderness: "Prepare the way of the LORD; Make straight in the desert A highway for our God... For the mouth of the LORD has spoken."*	**Fulfilled:** *And he went into all the region around the Jordan, preaching a baptism of repentance for the remission of sins, as it is written in the book of the words of Isaiah the prophet, saying: "The voice of one crying in the wilderness: 'Prepare the way of the LORD; Make His paths straight....And all flesh shall see the salvation of God.'"*

OLD TESTAMENT PROPHECY	FULFILLED BY CHRIST JESUS
Psalm 8:2	**Matthew 21:15**
Prophecy: Praises to God offended the enemy.	**Fulfilled:** *But when the chief priests and the teachers of the law saw the wonderful things he did and the children shouting in the temple courts, "Hosanna to the Son of David," they were indignant.*
Through the praise of children and infants you have established a stronghold against your enemies, to silence the foe and the avenger.	
Psalm 22:1	**Matthew 27:46**
Prophecy: The Messiah will cry out to God the Father, on the cross.	**Fulfilled:** *About three in the afternoon Jesus cried out in a loud voice, "Eli, Eli, lema sabachthani?" (which means "My God, My God, why have You forsaken Me?")*
My God, my God, why have you forsaken me? Why are you so far from saving me, so far from my cries of anguish.	

OLD TESTAMENT PROPHECY	FULFILLED BY CHRIST JESUS
Genesis 3:15 **Prophecy:** The Messiah will come from the Seed of a woman. *And I will put enmity between you and the woman, and between your offspring and hers; he will crush your head, and you will strike his heel.*	**Galatians 4:4-5** **Fulfilled:** *But when the set time had fully come, God sent his Son, born of a woman, born under the law, to redeem those under the law, that we might receive adoption to sonship.*
Micah 5:2 **Prophecy:** The Messiah will come out of the tribe of Judah. *"But you, Bethlehem Ephrathah, though you are small among the clans of Judah, out of you will come for me one who will be ruler over Israel, whose origins are from of old, from ancient times."*	**Luke 2:4-5** **Fulfilled:** *So Joseph also went up from the town of Nazareth in Galilee to Judea, to Bethlehem the town of David, because he belonged to the house and line of David. He went there to register with Mary, who was pledged to be married to him and was expecting a child.*

OLD TESTAMENT PROPHECY	FULFILLED BY CHRIST JESUS

Jeremiah 31:15

Prophecy: Mass murdering of innocent children at the time of Christ's birth, in order to kill the baby, Christ, as a child.

This is what the LORD says: "A voice is heard in Ramah, mourning and great weeping, Rachel weeping for her children and refusing to be comforted, because they are no more."

Matthew 2: 16-18

Fulfilled:
When Herod realized that he had been outwitted by the Magi, he was furious, and he gave orders to kill all the boys in Bethlehem and its vicinity who were two years old and under, in accordance with the time he had learned from the Magi. Then what was said through the prophet Jeremiah was fulfilled: "A voice is heard in Ramah, weeping and great mourning, Rachel weeping for her children and refusing to be comforted, because they are no more."

OLD TESTAMENT PROPHECY	FULFILLED BY CHRIST JESUS
Isaiah 50:6 **Prophecy:** The Messiah will endure much suffering and mockery from others. *I offered my back to those who beat me, my cheeks to those who pulled out my beard; I did not hide my face from mocking and spitting.*	**Matthew 26:67-68** **Fulfilled:** *Then they spit in his face and struck him with their fists. Others slapped him and said, "Prophesy to us, Messiah. Who hit you?"*
Isaiah 9:7 **Prophecy:** The Messiah will be an heir to David's throne. *Of the greatness of his government and peace there will be no end. He will reign on David's throne and over his kingdom, establishing and upholding it with justice and righteousness from that time on and forever. The zeal of the LORD Almighty will accomplish this.*	**Luke 1:32-33** **Fulfilled:** *He will be great and will be called the Son of the Most High. The Lord God will give him the throne of his father David, and he will reign over Jacob's descendants forever; his kingdom will never end.*

There are those critics of Jesus Christ who have come up with all kinds of theories, such as the fact that He "made these prophecies happen", by performing miracles, referring to Himself as the Messiah, etc, which are all ridiculous, because of certain circumstances surrounding these prophecies which Jesus Christ could not have controlled. Some examples of such circumstances, as recorded in the 4 Gospels include, but are not limited to (1) the place of His birth; (2) the rejection He experienced from others; (3) the beatings He experienced from the Roman soldiers; (4) the betrayal by Judas Iscariot ; (5) the mocking He endured from the Romans; (6) the abandonment He experienced when His disciples forsook Him and fled, etc, etc. I hope you can see why some of these critics are purely influenced by our enemy, Satan himself, who wants to keep people in bondage, thereby preventing them from receiving their salvation. How could Jesus Christ have controlled and manipulated how people treated Him during His pain, suffering and death? It was not possible!

Moreover, there are those critics who have said that these prophecies are mere coincidences. Again, how can this be? It is humanly impossible for one human being to fulfill **All** Messianic prophecies perfectly. These prophecies happened precisely, perfectly as prophesied in the Old Testament. Today we have so called "psychics" who are claiming to be able to predict the future. The difference is that most of their (referring to the psychics) predictions are usually generalized, vague, imprecise and based on certain foreknowledge.

In fact, most of the psychics are using human ability to predict the future; and for the most part, they are merely guessing based on what you tell them and based on current events, hence they are often wrong with their predictions. And most importantly, psychics' predictions cannot stand the test of time, because they are not supernatural.

On the other hand, in the case of Jesus Christ, the Old Testament prophecies or predictions are 100% precise, and perfectly accurate down to the tiniest details, as noted in the Old Testament, such as the fact that (1) " *they would pierce His side*" (Zechariah 12:10; see Matthew 27:9-10 on how it was fulfilled); (2) *"they casted lots with His clothes"* (Psalm 22:18; see Luke 23:34 on how it was fulfilled); (3) *"He would be betrayed with exactly 30 pieces of Silver and the money would be used to buy a potter's field"* (Zechariah 11:12-13; see Matthew 27:5-7 on how it was fulfilled); (4) *"His bones would not be broken"* (Psalm 34:20; see John 19:33-34 on how it was fulfilled), etc, etc! All these prophecies were fulfilled perfectly.

In essence, the above prophecies, plus much more that I could not discuss in this brief chapter, could not have come to pass without God's involvement — He indeed sent the Messiah into the world. Additionally, unlike psychics' predictions, these prophecies about the Messiah have stood the test of time and have passed with flying colors, 100% : Jesus Christ is indeed the Messiah!

Do you believe that Christ Jesus is the Messiah? If Yes, have you asked Him to come into your life? If No, I recommend that you do so, right now. He is the Messiah who died for your sins. Are you ready to make Him your personal Lord and Savior? If Yes, simply ask Him to come into your life right now, and He will accept. If you need help doing so, go back and reread chapter 1 of this book, and then say that simple prayer out loud, inviting Jesus Christ into your life now. It will be the best decision you will ever make in your life, and you will be very pleased!

....

IS JESUS CHRIST THE ONLY WAY TO THE ONLY ONE GOD?

Question # 4: Is Jesus Christ Really the Only Way?

Answer: Yes, because He fulfilled All prophecies and met God's holy standards 100%.

The Lord Jesus Himself explicitly made this claim, that no one can come to God the Father apart from Him. It is unfortunate that today, some critics of the Bible, are asserting that the followers of Jesus Christ made this claim and not the Lord Jesus Himself. But, Jesus Christ Himself said:

"I am the way and the truth and the life. No one comes to the Father except through me" (John 14:6), (emphasis author's).

Also, remember how, in chapter one 1 discussed that God is Holy and cannot fellowship with Mankind in his "fallen and unholy state"? Hopefully you recall! Here is the deal.

Because of God's holiness, He gave the Nation of Israel His holy and righteous laws for them to abide to in order to approach Him. God gave these Laws through the Old Testament Saint Moses, who acted as an intermediary and intercessor on their behalf. These laws included spiritual, moral, social and legislative laws.

Besides the 10 commandments as stated in Exodus chapter 20, there were over 600 such laws for the Jews to live by daily. Although the social and legislative laws primarily pertained to the Jewish Nation, the spiritual and moral components of the laws applied to all human beings, the entire human race, and they are still applicable to us today. These laws given to the Jews reflected God's holy character, and the Israelites were to reflect God's holy character to the other nations of the world, because they were God's chosen people (see Exodus chapter 19).

The problem was that, since God's laws are 100% holy and righteous, the Jews could not keep them 100%, hence it brought much guilt, shame, and condemnation to them (see 2 Corinthians chapter 3), and highlighted their need for a Messiah, to deliver them from the bondage of the Old Testament laws. And without the Messiah to deliver them from these laws, their Sinful Nature, and from the evil one, Satan himself, they could not satisfy God's perfect standards of holiness, nor approach Him on their own merit with their "fallen" Sinful Nature. The Jews were quite aware that " The Messiah" would someday deliver them; it had been predicted in the Old Testament.

Well, Jesus Christ was that Messiah, who fulfilled **All** of God's righteous and holy laws perfectly, and He never sinned; no human being in the history of the world has ever done this, and will ever do it, it has already been done. Once the Lord Jesus fulfilled All of the Scriptures through His sinless life, death and resurrection, God's wrath against sin (i.e., that transgression that Adam and Eve made) was satisfied 100%. God is no longer at "war" or angry with the human race because of the sin issue. As such, anyone who desires a relationship with the true living God of the Bible must come through His Only Son, Jesus Christ, Whose righteousness, we, as Christians, have inherited (i.e., imputed to us) at the time of our salvation, in our brand new "DNA", our regenerated "born again" spirits (Romans 3:22-24). When we approach God, we must approach Him only in the name of Jesus Christ, because God sees us through Christ as righteous and regenerated.

Thus, Jesus Christ is The Only Way to the Only True living God, because He has made us righteous in God's "eyes", and His precious blood purchased or redeemed us from that Sinful Nature inherited from Adam and Eve, and from the evil one, Satan. So YES, Jesus Christ is The Only Way to God. All other religious leaders such as Buddha, Muhammad, Krishna, Chinese Religious leaders, etc, including any upcoming religious leaders were, and are all "fallen" human beings, with their inherited Sinful Natures, making it impossible for them to approach The Holy and Righteous God on their own merit without Christ Jesus. These people cannot save you, only Jesus Christ offers us this hope to approach God, because He kept God's holy standards 100%.

So, do not be deceived, you cannot approach God apart from Jesus Christ. This is your eternity at balance; you will die someday, so make a decision for Christ today. If you sincerely desire to know God; you must, independently accept His Only one time sacrifice, Jesus Christ, then you will be able to have a relationship with The Only True God: The God of the Bible.

This Jesus Christ, The Messiah, is ready to come into your life right now! Are you ready to invite Him into your life as your personal Lord and Savior? If yes, simply ask Him, right now, and He will accept your invitation.

....

WHY DID JESUS CHRIST HAVE TO DIE TO ATONE FOR OUR SINS?

Question # 5: Why did Jesus Christ have to die to atone for our sins?

Answer: God is 100% holy, and sin cannot abide in His presence. Also, God is just, thus sin has to be dealt with justly; and in God's Laws, blood has to be shed for sins to be forgiven, period!

Most of the times, the "why" questions are not the right questions to ask, because these type of questions are delving into God's territory. I only include this question here because it is a very popular question, even among Christians, so I will provide a very succinct answer, and for those of you who want details, you can ask God this specific question yourself when you meet Him. Notwithstanding, there are things that we must accept by faith, and trust God with the answer. Also, there is a general rule that when the Bible is silent in certain areas, we have to be true to the Scriptures and be silent as well, lest we will speak incorrectly.

Nonetheless, with regards to this question at hand, God has given us some clues in His Scriptures, that can shed some light to the answer. The Bible teaches us that God is love; He does not give love, He is love in His nature. When God loves, He does not make a decision to love, He loves because that is His core nature: Love. He is also perfectly holy, righteous, and just. Since God is holy, it means that sin cannot abide in His presence. And since He is just in His nature or essence, it means that He has to carry out justice against sin. Most people like the fact that God is love, but they do not want to hear about His justice. Well, for God to be love, it means He has to hate evil; and since He is just, His punishment has to be just. I hope you are following this logic here.

The Bible teaches that the wages of sin is death, this is how God has to deal with sin (Romans 6:23). Why death? Because God takes the issue of sin seriously. Also, the Bible teaches us that without the shedding of blood, there is no forgiveness of sins (Hebrews 9:22). So in God's laws, blood has to be shed for sins to be atoned for, because the punishment of sin is death.

And we see this pattern of God's punishment for sins and His forgiveness through the shedding of blood evident throughout the Old Testament, where animal sacrifice was made for the sins of the Israelites to be forgiven. There was even the Day of Atonement as recorded in the book of Leviticus chapter 16, when the High Priest, Aaron, entered the most holy of holies and offered the perfect, spotless animal sacrifice , in order for the sins of the Israelite community to be forgiven, including his own sins. Even in dealing with the children of Israel, the Scriptures teach how Moses offered animal sacrifice to cleanse them from their sins (see the book of Exodus). So yes, the precious and sinless blood of our Lord Jesus had to be sacrificed for the sins of the entire human race to be atoned for, in accordance with God's laws, as revealed in the Scriptures.

Christ Jesus, God's sacrificial lamb, was offered on the cross on your behalf, so that you can have a relationship with God, the Father. All of your sins have been forgiven! Have you accepted God's sacrifice to you by faith? Have you asked the Lord Jesus to come into your life and make you a brand new person? If Yes, great! If No, I recommend that you seriously consider making that decision today! Tomorrow is not guaranteed to anyone!

Before you go to bed tonight, be certain you have the assurance of what will happen to you, if you were to die in your sleep. This is not meant to scare you, but it happens every day — people die in their sleep! If you are ready to ask Jesus Christ to come into your life, you can make that decision right now. If you need help praying, go back to chapter 1 and reread out loud, that simple prayer, asking Jesus to come into your life, and He will accept you, right now!

....

CHAPTER 6

DID JESUS REALLY DIE ON THE CROSS?

Question # 6: Did Jesus Really Die on the Cross?

Answer: YES, He died on the cross!

This is an interesting question, which most Christians find surprising to hear. But, believe it or not, there are various religious groups, specifically some Muslims, who hold to the notion that Jesus Christ did not really die on the cross. Here is why: If they can prove that the Lord Jesus never really died on the cross, then, they will be able to debunk the entire Christian faith and call it a hoax. Think about this for a minute: If Jesus Christ did not die on the cross, it means that no resurrection took place, which means our sins have not been atoned for. Additionally, this will mean that, we, as Christians, are just like any other world religion, believing in a lie, and also that we are still in bondage to our Sinful Nature, and to the devil; essentially, we are useless spiritually. But, YES, Jesus Christ died on the cross; He was resurrected, and our sins have been forgiven 100%. We, as true followers of Jesus Christ have been given a new nature, a regenerated spirit, and our names have been written in the Lamb's Book of Life (Revelation 20:12)! Hallelujah!

Anyone who disputes the fact that Jesus Christ actually died on that cross is just outright stupid, in my opinion; deceived, or blatantly denying this Truth, which is even consistent with modern medicine. As an experienced Health Care Provider for over a dozen years, it will take several chapters for me to argue, and to discuss the medical evidence to support the death of Jesus Christ on the cross, but space limitation does not provide me with that luxury in this book. So I will be very brief here.

Firstly, Jesus Christ endured hours of the most gruesome beatings (i.e., at least 39 lashes on His entire body) from the Roman soldiers, which led to several lacerations to His skin, muscles, and throughout His physical body, with subsequent severe hemorrhage (i.e., blood loss), causing gross fatigue and exhaustion. Without medical intervention, no human being could endure such massive hemorrhage, they would die within a few hours or days. The bleeding alone, with the amount of blood that Jesus Christ lost, with no medical attention, was a perfect set up for His death, right away, even before He was crucified. History tells us that the Roman soldiers used whips that were made of strong leather thongs to flog their victims, after stripping them of their clothes, and tying them to a post; this was brutal. This was what happened to the Lord Jesus. This type of trauma to the body is a death sentence, in and of itself.

Secondly, crucifixion has been described as the most

dehumanizing method to kill a person. During crucifixion, the condemned individual would experience severe difficulty breathing, because he or she would have to inhale and exhale while hanging from the cross with the hands lifted upward, making it almost impossible to breathe in that position. Thus, the ultimate cause of death during crucifixion was suffocation due to difficulty breathing.

Well, the act of breathing alone, in that position of hanging, plus the bleeding from the beatings and hanging with the nails on the hands of the individual would bring about death in a few hours. Medically speaking, it would be impossible to survive such an ordeal, and the body would go into a shock. Hence, while hanging on the cross, Jesus Christ suffered unbelievable pain, difficulty breathing, fatigue, exhaustion, and suffocation. He could not have survived the cross— impossible! He died on that cross, period!

Thirdly, when the Roman soldiers pierced the side of our Lord's body, there was the splitting of water and blood which came out of His body (John 19:34), which was a clear indication of a sign of death, consistent with strong medical evidence, due to major clotting of the major arteries. If Jesus Christ was not dead when that spear was thrust into His body, the Roman soldiers would have observed a strong flow of blood out of His body instead, but that was not the case, because He was already dead.

Fourthly, it was the custom of the Roman soldiers to break the legs of the individuals who were crucified, in order to ascertain a speedy death. But, the Holy Scripture tells us that

"The soldiers therefore came and broke the legs of the first man who had been crucified with Jesus, and then those of the other. But when they came to Jesus and found that he was already dead, they did not break his legs" (John 19:32-33), (emphasis author's).

In my view, based on the brief discussion in this chapter and the medical evidence presented, I believe it will take more faith to believe that Jesus Christ did not die on the cross. But indeed, He did die on that cross for your individual sins.

Jesus dying on that cross has paved the way for you to have a relationship with God the Father. And if you are willing, He is ready to come into your heart, right now (Revelation 3:20).

And, most unfortunately, some individuals erroneously believe that it was someone else who died on the cross, and not Jesus Christ Himself. This is a ridiculous deception from the enemy. I have this question for those of you who are still believing this lie: *What about the visible scars on Jesus' body that He showed one of His disciples, Thomas, who doubted His resurrection?* (John 20:24-27). So, what do you think?

Jesus Christ loves you, and He desires a personal relationship with you today, right now. Give Him a chance, and you will not regret it. By faith, simply invite Him into your life as your personal Lord and Savior, and He will change your life for the best!

....

DID JESUS REALLY RISE FROM THE DEAD?

Question # 7: Did Jesus Really Rise from the Dead?

Answer: Yes, Jesus Christ was raised from the dead as prophesied; He is alive, right now!

There are many critics of Christianity who have denied that the resurrection ever took place. I have often wondered why this is so difficult for some people to "swallow". God is the absolute "Boss"; He is Sovereign; He is the Creator of the heavens and the earth!

Can anything be impossible for Him? Of course the answer is NO. As such, it is my belief that those who deny the resurrection are willfully denying it because if they choose to accept that this historical event took place, which, indeed happened, then, they would have to make a decision to accept Christ as their Lord and Savior, and they do not want to do that. Thus, they must deny the resurrection and live in gross self denial as a coping mechanism, which is futile, anyway.

Firstly, how do I know the resurrection took place? Because (1) the Bible tells me it happened. And since the Bible is the Only proven, verifiable, infallible, inspired and authenticated Word of God compared to all other so called Sacred Books such as the Koran, the Jehovah's Witnesses and the Mormons Scriptures which are all unverifiable, (to be discussed later), etc, I trust the Bible's account of the resurrection 100%.

Secondly, over 500 eye witnesses saw the "Risen Christ", meaning, He appeared to these people after He rose from the dead. The Apostle Paul, a former persecutor of Christians saw the "Risen Christ", and that encounter changed his life dramatically, 180 degrees (see Acts chapter 9). The Apostle Paul went from being a persecutor of Christians, to a devout follower of Christ, the one whom God used to write over 50% of the New Testament under the inspiration of the Holy Spirit. Here is what the Apostle Paul wrote about the "Risen Christ", under the inspiration of the Holy Spirit.

For what I received I passed on to you as of first importance: that Christ died for our sins according to the Scriptures, that he was buried, that he was raised on the third day according to the Scriptures, and that he appeared to Cephas, and then to the Twelve. After that, he appeared to more than five hundred of the brothers and sisters at the same time, most of whom are still living, though some have fallen asleep. Then he appeared to James, then to all the apostles, and last of all he appeared to me also, as to one abnormally born (1 Corinthians 15:3-8).

Thirdly, Christ appeared to His disciples, as you can read from the Scriptural text above. These disciples, who were weak, fearful men before their encounter with the "Risen Christ," became bold and fearless men filled with the Holy Spirit, and spread the Gospel of Christ rapidly during the First Century. Moreover, with the exception of the Apostle John who died a natural death, Church history tells us that all of the apostles, including Paul himself, were martyred (i.e., killed) for their strong faith after their encounters with the "Risen Christ."

He Is Alive

Many individuals have died believing a lie because they were deceived, but who would die knowingly, for a lie? No sane person would do such a thing, right? These disciples were very willing to die for the Truth about Christ's resurrection, because they knew 100% that He was alive, and will welcome them into His kingdom!

Another interesting thing is that in spite of the harsh persecution about their faith, none of the apostles recanted their stories (i.e., denied that the resurrection happened) about their encounters with the "Risen Christ"! If the resurrection did not happen, just based on human nature, it is certain that one of the apostles or others who claimed to have seen the "Risen Christ" would have recanted, but none of them did. This is a critical factor to consider, because given enough pressure, most individuals would "crack" (i.e., recant or take back their statements). But in the case of the resurrection, not a single person did! Whao! You know why? Because, it did indeed happen!

Another thing to keep in mind is that the resurrection had such a profound impact on the Jews who later became followers of Christ, to the extent that, it changed the day of their gathering/worship from Saturdays to Sundays. They started worshiping together as a Church on Sundays because it was the day Christ rose from the dead. This was a significant change for the Jews, as it would have warranted severe punishment in accordance with the Mosaic Laws of the Old Testament. But, these Jews, who became ardent followers of Christ, believed in the "Risen Christ," and risked their lives because they could no longer adhere to the dos and don'ts of the Old Testament Laws: **Christ had fulfilled them All**!

All sorts of theories abound from critics about the resurrection. Some of these include, but are not limited to lies such as: (1) the Lord's disciples stole His body (this is common among the Jews); (2) someone else died on the cross and not Jesus Christ Himself (this is common among the Muslims); (3) the whole resurrection thing is a myth or a legendary story (this is common among atheists or agnostics); (4) the disciples experienced a hallucination; etc; etc. These are all unbelievably ridiculous theories, which pose more problems to explain, even by those who hold firm to these theories.

As an example, experts in the field of hallucination and hypnosis, such as psychiatrists and psychologists can verify that it is not possible for over 500 people to experience the exact type or manner of hallucination (in this case, seeing the "Risen Christ") over the same period of time. Also, the over 500 eye witnesses who saw the "Risen Christ" were in touch with reality, mentally sound, and did not even fit medical criteria of individuals who would experience hallucinations. Experts in the field of hallucination would agree that hallucinations can primarily happen within the context of certain medical diagnoses, such as schizophrenia, bipolar, paranoia delusional disorders, etc (Diagnostic & Statistical Manual of Mental Disorders, 5th Edition).

These people, over 500 eye witnesses, could not have all experienced a mental disorder at the same time, right? Common sense tells us that the answer is NO. Boy! In my opinion, this argument about hallucination is the most stupid of all; medically speaking, it does not make sense, as all these eye witnesses could not have experienced the exact same kind of hallucination about the "Risen Christ"! Does that make any sense to you?

In spite of the above weak , unverifiable and nonsensical arguments against the resurrection, the body of evidence for the resurrection absolutely speaks for itself, such as (1) the empty tomb; (2) the Roman guards that fled from the grave site once they noticed that the Lord's body was not there (the Roman guards guarding the Lord's tomb fled in fear of execution); (3) the large stone protecting the tomb was removed; (4) the empty grave clothes found in the empty tomb; (5) the eye witness accounts; etc; etc. All this body of evidence presents an undeniable, irrefutable, and proven evidence against those who are vehemently refusing that our Lord and Savior, Jesus Christ, is indeed Risen! Yes, indeed, Jesus Christ did rise from the dead! He was resurrected and is alive today, right now!

Do you have a personal relationship with Him? If not, I recommend that you do so – He will change your destiny permanently, for the best!

....

WAS JESUS CHRIST A REAL PERSON OR A LEGEND?

Question # 8: Was Jesus Christ a Real Person or a legend?

Answer: Jesus Christ was a real person who lived in time and space on this earth. He was not, and is not a legend!

This question may seem shocking to some of you, but there are many individuals who believe that Christ Jesus never really existed, that He was a legend, made up by Christians to support their beliefs. In fact, sometime last month, one of my patients informed me that she was having a very difficult time witnessing to her neighbor, because this neighbor believes that Christ was not a real person who lived on this earth; hence, yes, many people think this way. So how do we know that Jesus Christ actually existed? We know primarily because God tells us so in the Bible, and the Bible is God's Only inspired, infallible and verifiable Word to us.

Then, besides the Bible, there are numerous historical evidence that agree with the existence of our Lord Jesus Christ in time and space, on this earth. Since the Bible gives us historical accounts of the history of the earth, it is therefore very appropriate to evaluate non-biblical historical data for accuracy and consistency with biblical events. Keep in mind that non-biblical historical data cannot validate whether or not the Holy Scripture is inspired by God; however, they can validate Scriptural accounts of events as revealed in the Bible.

To illustrate, I am now writing this book in the year 2017, and the President of the United States of America is President Donald Trump. Currently, there are various historians, during this present time, who will be writing about the president, and these writings will possibly be preserved for further generations, right? Likewise, historians who existed during or close to the era when our Lord lived on this earth wrote extensively about Him. However, because of poor technology back then, all of the records were not preserved, but some were, which can help us to validate what the Bible already tells us, that Jesus Christ existed in time and space as a real person.

As an example, non-biblical writings such as from famous First Century historian Josephus Flavus, mentioned Jesus Christ in his writings, thus validating the fact that He was a real human being who existed in time and space on this earth. As an example, below is a statement from famous Jewish historian Flavus Josephus, validating the existence of our Lord Jesus as an individual who lived on this earth in time and space:

"... there was about this time Jesus, a wise man, if it be lawful to call him a man; for he was a doer of wonderful works, a teacher of such men as receive the truth with pleasure. He drew over to him both many of the Jews and many of the Gentiles. He was [the] Christ. And when Pilate, at the suggestion of the principal men amongst us, had condemned him to the cross, those that loved him at the first did not forsake him; for he appeared to them alive again the third day; as the divine prophets had foretold these and ten thousand other wonderful things concerning him. And the tribe of Christians, so named from him, are not extinct at this day...."

(Antiquities of the Jews, 18: 63).

Other noted non-biblical writings about Christians and the Lord Jesus included but are not limited to those from (1) the Jewish Talmud, which is a collection of Jewish customs, laws and traditions; (2) writings from the early Church Leaders/Fathers such as Ignatius who died around (A.D. 108); Eusebius who died around (A.D. 339); etc; (3) other writers such as Thallus (A.D. 52); Julius Africanus (A.D. 221); and (4) other writings from Roman historians such as Tacitus (A.D. 115); etc, all mentioned Christ Jesus in their writings. All these writings validate biblical accounts of Christ as a person in the history of the world.

It is interesting that if you were to ask the average person whether or not Julius Caesar or Plato lived and existed on this earth purely based on historical account, they would respond by saying: YES. Also, if you were to ask most people if George Washington ever existed in time and space, based on history, they would say YES, even though they have never seen these people. But when it comes to Jesus Christ, some people question His existence. In fact, most people are not even aware that there are more documented non-biblical writings (i.e., historical writings) about the existence of Jesus Christ, compared to other noted historical individuals, such as Julius Caesar and Plato.

Whether you accept it or not, our Lord and Savior, Jesus Christ, was a real person who lived in time and space on this earth, over 2000 years ago, with overwhelming evidence of His existence as a historical person. And today, this Jesus Christ, can change your life, if you are willing to accept Him into your heart. God has given you the Free Will to make that decision: I hope you choose wisely!

The unfortunate thing is this: your impression of Christ does not, and will never change the <u>absolute Truth that He was/is God, and without</u> <u>Him, you cannot have a relationship with the true</u> <u>living God.</u>

<u>Thus, you might as well consider His claims and make a decision to accept Him into your life today.</u>

Have you asked Him into your life yet? If no, why not? What are you waiting for? What are you considering? You do not have to earn a relationship with Him nor do you have to deserve it, none of us deserves it. Just receive His unconditional love for you and His forgiveness of your sins! By faith, you can receive His unfathomable love for you by asking Him to come into your life as your personal Lord and Savior, and He will, right this moment!

....

ARE THE JEHOVAH'S WITNESSES AND THE MORMONS REFERRING TO THE SAME JESUS CHRIST?

Question # 9: Are the Jehovah's Witnesses and the Mormons Referring to the same Jesus Christ?

Answer: NO, the Jehovah's Witnesses and the Mormons are not referring to, or calling upon the same Jesus Christ, as the true Christians do. As such, by their own doctrines, they are not true followers of the Lord Jesus Christ.

I want to begin by saying, straight away, that there is only One Jesus Christ, as revealed in the True Christian Bible — Jesus Christ the Messiah: 100% human being and 100% God. One thing is certain, Jesus Christ has fully revealed His true identity to the world, as described in the true Christian Bible. As discussed in previous chapters of this book, Jesus Christ was the Only Son of God; He was fully God and fully Man; and His other offices have already been discussed in chapter 1 of this book, refer there for details. Unfortunately, in their doctrines, the Jehovah's Witnesses and the Mormons reject the true claims of Jesus Christ, as He has fully revealed Himself to us in the Bible.

And according to Jesus Christ Himself, if anyone denies His works , claims, and true identity, then He will also reject that individual in front of God the Father (Matthew 10:33). Jesus Christ has left us with only two choices: accept Him completely or reject Him, no in-between.

A person cannot claim that he or she accepts Jesus Christ as the Messiah, but then rejects His claims as God; No, this is not acceptable by Jesus Christ Himself.

Under the inspiration of the Holy Spirit, the Apostle John teaches us that anyone who denies that Jesus Christ came in the flesh (i.e., referring to the incarnation), is antichrist; that is to say, that individual has rejected Jesus Christ as the Messiah, period! Here is how the Apostle John explains it:

Dear friends, do not believe every spirit, but test the spirits to see whether they are from God, because many false prophets have gone out into the world. This is how you can recognize the Spirit of God: Every spirit that acknowledges that Jesus Christ has come in the flesh is from God, but every spirit that does not acknowledge Jesus is not from God. This is the spirit of the antichrist, which you have heard is coming and even now is already in the world (1 John 4:1-3), (emphasis author's).

Then, under the inspiration of the Holy Spirit, the Apostle John reiterated the same warning in His second epistle, here is what he said: *"I say this because many deceivers, who do not acknowledge Jesus Christ as coming in the flesh, have gone out into the world. Any such person is the deceiver and the antichrist"* (2 John 1:7), (emphasis author's).

In His wisdom, God has given us a guide, to help us to ascertain who really is a true follower of the Lord Jesus. I am certain that there are some individuals who might be thinking that I am being judgmental here; but, I am not. I am only espousing the Truth, right out of God's Word: The Bible. While the Jehovah's Witnesses and the Mormons might call upon the name of Jesus Christ, be warned, because these Christian cults (i.e., groups that deviate from God's Truths as taught in the Bible), have outrightly rejected the complete claims of Jesus Christ, and are unfortunately putting people into bondage and legalism (i.e., do's and don'ts), in the name of God, which is all false and wrong.

As you can see from the Scriptural texts above, a person's position about who Jesus Christ is, is the major criterion to evaluate whether or not the individual is a true follower of Christ (that is to say, a true Christian) or an antichrist. With this thought, let us briefly examine the Jehovah's Witnesses beliefs and/or position about Christ Jesus. There are several heresies (i.e., false teachings) in the Jehovah's Witnesses cult, but due to space limitation in this book, I am unable to expound on all of them. Thus, I will only focus on some of their false beliefs about Jesus Christ, which in and of themselves, exclude them as true Christians or followers of the Lord Jesus.

False Teachings about Christ by the Jehovah's Witnesses

The Jehovah's Witnesses

❖ Reject the Deity of Jesus Christ. They reject Jesus Christ as God Himself who came into this world in the flesh . Essentially, they deny the true biblical teachings of the incarnation. And remember that the Bible is very straight forward in teaching that anyone who denies the doctrine of the incarnation is an antichrist. Since this is the case, how can the Jehovah's Witnesses be true Christians? Thus, based on the teachings from the true Christian Bible, the Jehovah's Witnesses are not true Christians, which means they are not calling upon the name of the same Jesus Christ as true Christians do!

❖ Believe that Jesus Christ was inferior to God the Father. This erroneous belief is due in part because they reject the Deity of Christ, and only focus on His humanity. **The Jehovah's Witnesses believe that, "Jesus was only a perfect man, not God in flesh."** But as already explained, Jesus Christ, in His humanity (i.e., His nature as a human being), <u>humbled Himself unto the will of the Father, but His humility did not make Him less inferior to God the Father, in His Diety.</u>

❖ <u>Reject the biblical teaching of the Trinity. As true Christians, we worship One God, in three unique and</u>

distinct persons: God the Father, God the Son, and God the Holy Spirit, although 100% equal in divinity, authority and power. Although the word Trinity is not found in the Bible, the teachings are evident throughout the Scriptures, from the book of Genesis to the book of Revelation (e.g., see Genesis 1:26; Matthew 28:19; 2 Corinthians 13:14; 1 Peter 1:2; etc).

❖ Believe that Jesus Christ was a created being, **yet the true Christian Bible teaches that Jesus Christ is eternal, and has always existed, even before the creation of the universe. In fact, the Bible is so clear that Jesus Christ always existed**: He is the Alpha and the Omega (i.e., the beginning and the end), (Revelation 1:8) and through Christ, the entire universe was created (Colossians 1:17). So it is obvious, Jesus Christ was not and is not a created being!

❖ Believe that extra "works" are necessary for one's salvation, before the person is accepted by God, which is absolutely false. Essentially, they reject the complete work of Jesus Christ on the cross, yet Jesus Himself, on the cross said: **"It is finished!"** (John 19:30). What was finished? The work of salvation, which Jesus Christ completed on the cross 100%.

As for the Latter Day Saints, also known as the Mormon Church, their beliefs about Jesus Christ are just as false, and as contrary to what the true Christian Bible teaches about the real Jesus Christ Himself.

False Teachings about Christ by the Latter Day Saints (Mormons)

Here is what the Latter Day Saints, or the Mormons believe about Jesus Christ, which makes them antichrist, a pseudo Christian cult.

The Mormons

❖ Reject the Deity of Christ Jesus;

❖ Believe that Jesus Christ was a created human being;

❖ Believe that God was once a human being, like one of us. Yet, the true Christian Bible teaches that God is a Spirit (John 4:24), eternal, and has always existed, even before the creation of the universe (see the book of Genesis; Colossians, etc). This erroneous teachings are unbelievable; yet, Satan has deceived so many innocent people to believe these lies. It is so absurd that, it is best that I present some of the Mormons' core beliefs as quotations, right from their own teachings, for you to read for yourself.

Below are some of the false teachings from the Church of Mormons:

"God himself was once as we are now, and is an exalted man, and sits enthroned in yonder heavens! That is the great secret, if the veil were rent today, and the great God who holds this world in its orbit, and who upholds all worlds and all things by his power, was to make himself visible,--I say, if you were

to see him today, you would see him like a man in form--like yourselves in all the person, image, and very form as a man,"

(Teachings of the Prophet Joseph Smith, p. 345).

"We have imagined and supposed that God was God from all eternity. I will refute that idea, and take away the veil, so that you may see . . . yea, that God the Father of us all, dwelt on an earth, the same as Jesus Christ himself did, and I will show it from the Bible"

(Teachings of the Prophet Joseph Smith, pp. 345-346).

"That which is without body or parts is nothing. There is no God in heaven but that God who has flesh and bones"

(Teachings of Presidents of the Church--Joseph Smith, p. 42).

It is quite obvious that the above teachings from the Mormon Church disqualify them as true followers of the Lord Jesus Christ. There is no need for me to explain any further. You can see the heresies in their own teachings for yourself. I am still amazed that people would believe such nonsense about God, the Creator!

Just in case you are wondering how the Jehovah's Witnesses and the Mormons can continue to teach these lies, the answer is simple. Their sacred scriptures or so called New World Translation Bible, which is the main scripture for the Jehovah's Witnesses; and the Book of Mormons, for the Mormon Church, are both falsified, translated grossly incorrectly, with overwhelming distortions of the truths from the true Christian Bible, in order to support their false doctrines. There is only One True Holy Scriptures, the true Christian Bible.

The Jehovah's Witnesses Bible, Book of Mormons, and all other sacred scriptures of the various world religions made by man cannot all be true—only One can be true. You know why?

Because based on the simple Law of Contradiction or principle of Contradiction, two opposite or contradictory statements cannot both be true at the same time, one has to be wrong. So how do we know?

We know based on multiple factors such as various internal and external evidence validating or disproving the various Sacred books of the different world religions.

The good news is that, only the true Christian Bible has the internal and external evidence to support its claims, compared to all other sacred books in the history of the world.

I do not want to expound on this very relevant discussion, lest I would delve outside the focus of this book. But for those wanting more information about this, check the resource list at the end of this book to obtain my book titled "**Can I Trust the Bible?**", where I address these issues in details. Suffice it to say that, these pseudo Christian cults (i.e., the Jehovah's Witnesses and the Mormons) are teaching their false doctrines from falsified sacred books: no wonder their teachings are wrong!

Since both the Jehovah's Witnesses and the Mormons believe that Jesus Christ was a created being, I want to end this section with some Scriptures from the true Christian Bible, which highlight the Supremacy of Christ Jesus as The Creator, Who is eternal. The Apostle Paul wrote, under the inspiration of the Holy Spirit:

"The Son is the image of the invisible God, the firstborn over all creation. For in him all things were created: things in heaven and on earth, visible and invisible, whether thrones or powers or rulers or authorities; all things have been created through him and for him. He is before all things, and in him all things hold together. And he is the head of the body, the church; he is the beginning and the firstborn from among the dead, so that in everything he might have the supremacy. For God was pleased to have all his fullness dwell in him, and through him to reconcile to himself all things, whether things on earth or things in heaven, by making peace through his blood, shed on the cross" (Colossians 1:15-20), (emphasis author's).

To the Scriptural Truth above, we say: AMEN!

So do you know the "real" Jesus Christ of the true Christian Bible? If not, you can change that right now! Ask Him to come into your life as your personal Lord and Savior, and He will come and live in your heart by faith, right now.

....

WHAT IS JESUS CHRIST DOING RIGHT NOW?

Question #10: What is Jesus Christ doing right now?

Answer: Jesus Christ is in heaven. He has been exalted, and is seated at the right hand of God the Father, interceding on behalf of all of His true followers.

The earthly ministry of Jesus Christ was completed at His death, burial and resurrection. Before His crucifixion, death, resurrection and ascension into heaven, the Lord Jesus told His first Century disciples, including all His true followers today, that the Holy Spirit, Whom God the Father will send in His name, will be sent to the earth, to remind us of All things, including all of His teachings (John 14:26). The Lord went on to explain how it was better for Him to return to heaven; but the Holy Spirit, Who can be everywhere at the same time, will be with us forever, as our comforter and guide, to help us to live the Christian life (John 14:15-21).

Today, the Holy Spirit is the One reminding us of All things pertaining to the Lord Jesus, and the Lord Jesus' primary ministry today is that of our intercessor. After His sinless life, death and resurrection, the Lord fulfilled God's righteous laws perfectly, more than any other human being can and will ever do. As such, the Bible teaches that:

"Wherefore God also hath highly exalted him, and given him a name which is above every name: That at the name of Jesus every knee should bow, of things in heaven, and things in earth, and things under the earth; And that every tongue should confess that Jesus Christ is Lord, to the glory of God the Father" (Philippians 2:9-11), (emphasis author's).

Since His resurrection therefore, the Lord Jesus has been very busy with His ministry of intercession: *"Therefore he is able to save completely those who come to God through him, because he always lives to intercede for them"* (Hebrews 7:25). We are also told *"Who then is the one who condemns? No one. Christ Jesus who died—more than that, who was raised to life—is at the right hand of God and is also interceding for us"* (Romans 8:34), (emphasis author's).

Today, many Christians often forget that it is the Holy Spirit, the Spirit of Truth, Who is currently present in the world, right now, convicting the world of sin, righteousness, and judgment. That is to say, the Holy Spirit is the One proving that the "world" is wrong about sin, and He convicts the sinner, leading him or her to repentance, if he or she desires to do so (John 16:8). The Holy Spirit is also the One bringing into our remembrance, the awesome ministry of our Lord and Savior Jesus Christ.

So the Lord Jesus Himself is currently exercising His role as our mediator, interceding for All of His true followers to God the Father; and He is expected to return to His earth soon, to rule someday as King of Kings and Lord of Lords! So next time you call upon the name of the Lord Jesus, remember that it is the Holy Spirit working through you, enabling you to remember the awesome works of your Lord and Savior Jesus Christ, and of His presence!

So, I have a question for you: Has the Holy Spirit been speaking to your heart about accepting Jesus Christ as your personal Lord and Savior? I am certain that He has, because it is God's will that you accept His free gift to you, Jesus Christ. Thus, if you have not yet responded to that still voice in your heart, you can do so right now, by asking Jesus Christ to come into your life as your personal Lord, Savior, and friend, and He will accept.

CHAPTER 11

QUESTION # 11: DID JESUS CHRIST REALLY BELIEVE IN THE WORD OF GOD AS WRITTEN IN THE BIBLE?

Question # 11: Did Jesus Christ Really Believe in the Word of God as written in the Bible?

Answer: Yes, He did 100%.

This is an interesting question, which some of you may find laughable. But it is indeed a very valid question, especially because there are those who claim to be followers of Jesus Christ, yet reject All of the teachings in the Bible as the final authority for their lives. I have often wondered, "how can anyone say Jesus is their Lord and Savior, yet refuse to uphold the Bible as the final authority for the Christian's life?" Nonetheless, Yes, Jesus Christ believed in God's Word 100%. You may wonder how and why. Here are some obvious reasons: He authenticated the Holy Scriptures by quoting from it throughout His earthly ministry; He fulfilled All Scriptures as already discussed; He was the eternal Word of God that was supernaturally made flesh. Let us briefly examine these closely:

Jesus Christ Authenticated the Holy Scriptures:

The Lord Jesus was the Word of God in action. In essence, He was a "walking" Word of God, and a display for all who saw Him. He perfectly exemplified how to live purposefully, and practically through the Holy Scriptures.

℠ Firstly, the Lord Jesus authenticated the Scriptures through many ways. He quoted from the Old Testament Scriptures throughout His ministry (e.g., Matthew 13: 14-15, 15: 8-9; 21:16, etc);

℠ Secondly, He pointed others to search the Scriptures to find out that He was indeed the Messiah (see John 5:39-40). Jesus Christ called Himself the Messiah (see chapter 1 of this book). By doing this, He authenticated the Old Testament Scriptures, which taught that the Messiah was to come;

℠ Thirdly, Christ Jesus Himself said He came into the earth to fulfill All of God's Laws (Matthew 5:17-18);

℠ Fourthly, the Lord Jesus affirmed the permanency of Scripture, and thus authenticated it when He simply stated: *"Heaven and earth shall pass away, but my words shall not pass away"* (Matthew 24:35);

℠ Fifthly, Jesus Christ relied on the Holy Scripture as the primary way to overcome Satan when He was tempted in the wilderness (Matthew 4:1-11). Hence, He showed His followers how to practically apply the Word of God into their lives daily, thus setting a precedence for using God's Word as the best antidote (i.e., the Only Truth) against the lies from our enemy, Satan.

The Lord's Prophecies

Another way that the Lord Jesus authenticated the Holy Scripture was through His prophecies, which came to pass 100% as prophesied. Below are just a few examples:

- ꙮ The Lord prophesied that one of His disciples, Peter, would deny Him three times (Luke 22:31-34), and it happened exactly as prophesied (Luke 22:54-62);

- ꙮ The Lord prophesied that one of His disciples, Judas Iscariot would betray Him, and it happened exactly as prophesied (Matthew 26: 14-25, 47-50; 27: 1-10);

- ꙮ Jesus Christ prophesied about the destruction of the Temple and Jerusalem (Luke 21:5-24), and it happened precisely, in 70 AD;

- ꙮ The Lord prophesied that He would be raised from the dead after three days , and indeed, He rose from the dead exactly on the third day (Matthew 26:26-32; 28: 1-20);

- ꙮ The Lord prophesied that all of His disciples would flee and abandon Him once He was arrested (Matthew 26: 31-32), and it came to pass precisely as He stated (Matthew 26:56), etc, etc.

There are many other such prophecies of the Lord, but I do not have the space in this book to elaborate on all of them. Suffice it to say that, the Lord was actually writing the Holy Scriptures through His prophecies that all came to pass perfectly, thus providing a 100% confirmation that the Word of God is God's inspired, infallible and inerrant Holy Scripture, which Jesus Christ Himself believed in, and relied on completely, throughout His earthly ministry!

Additionally, here is what Jesus Christ Himself said about His Words, which are considered 100% Scripture:

"The Spirit gives life; the flesh counts for nothing. The words I have spoken to you—they are full of the Spirit and life (John 6:63), (emphasis author's).

Obviously, the Lord believed that His own Words are the Only source of real life, right! Then He added that anyone who practices His Words (i.e., His teachings in the Scriptures), will be basing his or her life on a solid foundation, which will not crumble in times of calamities and hardships in this present life (Matthew 7:24-27). So yes, Jesus Christ did believe in the Bible as God's Word 100%. What about you? Do you believe in the infallibility of God's Word? If yes, do you put it to practice in your life daily? If no, why not?

And if you believe in the Bible, have you accepted Jesus Christ as the Messiah? If not, by faith, you can genuinely ask Him right now to come into your heart and change you, and He will do so today!

C H A P T E R   1 2

....

WHAT HAPPENS WHEN I ACCEPT JESUS CHRIST AS MY PERSONAL LORD AND SAVIOR?

Question #12: What happens When I Accept Jesus Christ as my personal Lord and Savior?

Answer: If you genuinely accept Jesus Christ as your personal Lord and Savior, your "darkened" spirit is immediately regenerated; that is to say, "made alive," and you will instantly be "born again." You will then become a follower of Jesus Christ, a true Christian.

The Bible teaches that human beings are tripartite beings, consisting of a mind, body and a spirit, bound together as one (1 Thessalonians 5:23). According to the Bible, every human being is born into this world as a sinner (Romans 3:23) , because at the time of our birth, we inherit a Sinful Nature from our common ancestors Adam and Eve, who transgressed God's law, and as such, sin and death entered into the world (see Genesis chapter 3). As a result of this Sinful Nature, each human being needs a regenerated spirit from the living God, before he or she can fellowship with God Who is Holy.

81

Receiving this regenerated spirit is only possible when you accept Jesus Christ as your personal Lord and Savior, because He is the only **One** who has met God's perfect standards for holiness 100% and fulfilled All of God's laws perfectly.

The moment a person genuinely accepts Jesus Christ, he or she is instantly redeemed (i.e., purchased) from the Kingdom of darkness belonging to Satan, and from their Sinful Nature. This redemption takes place because of the sinless and precious blood of Jesus Christ; then the individual's darkened spirit is immediately regenerated, and he or she automatically experiences a spiritual "rebirth" or becomes "born again." Each human being experiences a physical birth, when the individual is birthed into this world. But for those who want to have a relationship with the true living God through Jesus Christ, a second type of birth in the spiritual realm, called "born again," is required, whereby God would give the individual a "new spirit," full of life.

You Become A New "Creature"

Once a person is born again, he or she is immediately sealed with the Holy Spirit (Ephesians 1:13), and many other things happen simultaneously in the spiritual realm, causing the individual to become a new creature (2 Corinthians 5:17), or essentially a brand new person, with a brand new "DNA," spiritually, and we accept all of these by faith, based on God's Word. For those of you interested in further studies about your new identity in Christ, I recommend that you check the resource list at the end of this book and obtain my book titled:

" **Are You Moving Forward with Jesus? How To Excel in Your Identity in Christ,**" where I discuss this in depth.

Briefly, at the time of accepting Jesus Christ as your personal Lord and Savior (i.e., at the time of your salvation), you are instantly reconciled into a relationship with God the Father, and you attain peace with God. Also, He forgives All of your sins, past, present and future sins (Hebrews 9:26, see Hebrews chapter 10), and absolves you from all of the punishment from your sins (i.e., you are justified) (Romans 5:1); and you are made righteous, that is to say, you attain good moral and spiritual standing with God, because of your relationship with Christ Jesus (Romans 3:22; 2 Corinthians 5:21). These are all of the blessings you have inherited in Christ by faith (see Ephesians chapters 1 and 2).

Much more, you become a child of God, and He adopts you as one of His precious children, and then sends His Spirit into your heart, thus you can call God your Father (Galatians 4:6).

As God's child, you become joint heirs with Christ Jesus Himself, meaning, anything that belongs to Jesus Christ is now yours. You have His joy, peace, freedom from the Kingdom of darkness, prosperity in every area of life, etc. Essentially, by becoming a Christian, you inherit all of God's Kingdom through faith in Christ: This is your new identity in Christ! This is an amazingly awesome news! Hallelujah!

As already mentioned, all of the above changes happen in the spiritual realm. But to experience these changes in the physical realm, you have to (1) believe and accept them by faith; and (2) abide in Jesus Christ daily (i.e., stay connected, rooted, and attached to Christ, and practice His teachings), in order for the life in your spirit to radiate to the physical realm. And as you abide in Christ and diligently study the Word of God and put it to practice daily while living in obedience, the Fruit of God's Spirit: love, joy, peace, patience, kindness, goodness, faithfulness, gentleness and self-control (Galatians 5: 22-23), will start emanating out of you and others will take notice.

If you have never made a genuine confession to accept Jesus Christ as your personal Lord and Savior, I want to give you the opportunity to do so, right now. The Bible teaches that if you believe in your heart that Jesus Christ is Lord, God Himself in the flesh, Who died for your sins, was buried, but then was resurrected on the third day, you will become born again (Romans 10:17).

Jesus Christ fulfilled All of God's holy standards perfectly, like already discussed, something that no other human being in the history of the world has ever done and will ever do. As such, there is no other name given unto Mankind by which salvation must be attained, except through Jesus Christ (Acts 4:12). He is your only ticket to life. He is The Way, The Truth and The Life (John 14:6). If you agree, and are ready to accept Jesus Christ into your life and you need help doing so, then say the simple prayer below, if you are genuine. Remember, the prayer does not save you; rather, it is what you believe in your heart, and you are just confessing out loud. Below is the prayer:

"Dear God, I thank you for sending Jesus Christ to die for all of my sins. Forgive me for not acknowledging this absolute Truth before. I am asking You, Lord Jesus, to come into my life, right now, and make me a new person. Today, I denounce all false gods in my life, and I have accepted You, Jesus Christ, as my personal Lord and Savior. Dear God, I ask that you fill me, right now, with Your Holy Spirit so that I can live the Christian life. By faith, I believe You have accepted me, and I am now a true follower of Jesus Christ. Thank you God, in Jesus name, AMEN."

If you said the above prayer genuinely, based on the authority of the Holy Bible, I declare you are now a true Christian. Welcome into God's Kingdom, the Kingdom of light. If you want, contact us, so that we can send you more teaching materials to help you grow in your journey with God through Christ, and the enabling of the Holy Spirit.

....

CAN I LOSE MY SALVATION IN CHRIST?

Question # 13: Can I lose my Salvation in Christ?

Answer: If it was a 100% genuine conversion, then No, you cannot lose your salvation.

This is an amazingly relevant question that often comes up among Christians, and has left many people fearful and in bondage. Hopefully, I can provide some clarity in this area to help you, if you are concerned about your salvation. There are those who are erroneously thinking that a true Christian can lose his or her salvation in Christ. This notion is unbelievably unscriptural and wrong, if it was a genuine conversion. This question requires a very elaborate discussion that I do not have the space to provide in this book; nonetheless, I will provide some major reasons why a true Christian cannot lose a genuine salvation in Christ.

Major Reasons Why You Cannot Lose Your Salvation

➢ Firstly, your salvation is 100% based on Christ Jesus' finished redemptive work on the cross. It is God's

FREE gift to you because of His grace (i.e., His unmerited favor towards us even though we do not deserve it), and by faith, you have accepted this FREE gift, that is to say, you have placed your faith in Jesus Christ as your personal Lord and Savior.

➢ Secondly, your salvation in Christ is not dependent on any of your actions or "good works". Jesus Christ did it all! Thus, since there is absolutely nothing you did to receive this FREE gift from God, except accept it by faith, there is absolutely nothing you can do to lose it, if it was genuine.

Here is where many people who believe you can lose your salvation go wrong — they erroneously associate salvation with "works" or "good actions", which is unscriptural. On the Cross, Jesus Christ said "It is finished" (John 19:30). There is no in-between with salvation.

Jesus Christ fulfilled God's perfect and righteous laws 100%; He did it all! Your good works in regards to your salvation will never be accepted by God. In fact, those who are depending on their good works plus what Jesus did on the cross in order to attain their salvation will never find "REST" in this life. This "works" righteousness mentality is an affront to God; you must come to Him through faith in Jesus Christ, and enter His rest by faith (see the book of Romans chapters 2,3,4; Galatians chapters 3 through 5; and the entire book of Hebrews).

I have actually counseled Christians who believe that the free gift of salvation is "too easy", as such, they struggle to accept that no "works" is required. Well, that is the grace of God. Yes, no works are required: This is God's unconditional love to us, sinners, even though we do not deserve it.

➢ Thirdly, the moment you become a true Christian, you are instantly sealed, permanently, with the Holy Spirit, guaranteeing your salvation (Ephesians 1:13). Nothing can break this permanent seal by the Holy Spirit, not even sin; although this is not an excuse for you to sin.

Besides, any true follower of the Lord Jesus desires to abstain from all sorts of sins, and to live a holy life pleasing to the Lord, as he or she allows the Holy Spirit to lead his or her life. There are those who erroneously believe that sin can cause someone to lose their salvation. The only way for a person to reason like this is when he or she categorizes sins as big or little sins.

But unfortunately, God does not categorize sin. In His eyes, sin is sin, period! There are no big and little sins, although the consequences may vary, but to God: sin is sin, period! Although sin cannot cause a true Christian to lose his or her salvation, sin will prevent God's presence in the individual's life, and open the door for the enemy, Satan, to devour you. So do not practice sin and abuse God's grace. Practicing sin will kill you before your time!

Here is another consideration about the notion that sin cannot cause a person to lose his or her salvation. Before you were even born into this world and heard of Jesus Christ for the first time, He had already died for your sins, and He was patiently waiting for one of His co-workers to share the good news with you, so that you would accept His sacrificial death and be saved, right? And since He only died once, and has forgiven all of your sins, past, present and future sins, how would sin cause you to lose your salvation? Is Jesus going to die again for your sins? Of course Not. Jesus only died once, He will never go through the pain, shame and humiliation a second time—He died for sins just once, you get the point? (See Hebrews chapter 10).

> Fourthly, God, in His foreknowledge, knows those who would, by their own choices, accept the sacrificial death and resurrection of His Son, Jesus Christ, and be saved. He also knows all those who would, by their own choice, reject Him, and send themselves to hell. But because of His love, He is continuously placing barriers in peoples' paths so that they do not send themselves to

hell. You may wonder how? By sending His coworkers here on the earth to continuously proclaim the Gospel message of Jesus Christ to everyone, giving each person the opportunity to change his or her destiny from hell into heaven. But unfortunately, because God has given each of us a Free Will, many individuals reject God's free gift to Mankind, Jesus Christ, and send themselves to hell, which is not God's will for anyone.

Additionally, as evidence that true converts to Christianity cannot lose their salvation, God has already predestined to conform them (i.e., all true Christians) into the image of His Son, Jesus Christ, through the sanctifying work (i.e., being set apart for God's use) of the Holy Spirit indwelling them (Romans 8: 28-29). This indwelling work of the Holy Spirit is progressive throughout the believer's earthly life, and the complete conformation is attained at the believer's death and union with the Lord. When God preordains something, it comes to pass, period! The process of sanctification is not interrupted; thus a person who is a true convert cannot lose his or her salvation in Christ.

➤ Fifthly, Jesus said something powerful, which confirms 100% that a person cannot lose his or her salvation in Christ. Here is what the Lord said about the fact that once you are His, no one will ever take you away from Him. He said: *"...My sheep listen to my voice; I know them, and they follow me. **I give them eternal life, and*** *they shall never perish; no one will snatch them out of my hand. My Father, who has given them to me, is greater than all ; no one can snatch them out of my Father's hand. I and the Father are one"* (John 10:25-30), (emphasis author's). The Lord Jesus has engraved you "in the palm of His hand", you are 100% secured in His hands! So relax!

➤ Sixthly, under the inspiration of the Holy Spirit, the Apostle John added that, all those who claim to have walked away from Christ were never His in the first place; they were never true converts, period! Here is how the Apostle penned it: *"They went out from us, but they were not of us; for if they had been of us, they would no doubt have continued with us: but they went out, that they might be made manifest that they were not all of us"* (1 John 2:19), (emphasis author's).

As you can see from the Apostle John's teaching, anyone who claimed to have lost his or her salvation in Christ never had a genuine encounter with the Lord Jesus in the first place.

A person's action of walking away from the Lord is a clear 100% sign that he or she never belonged to Him in the first place, lest they could have been sealed with the Holy Spirit, thus making it impossible for the person to walk away, and to lose his or her salvation. So no, a person cannot lose a genuine salvation in Christ.

An Often Misunderstood Passage of Scripture

I am very aware that some people hold to the notion that individuals can lose their salvation based on the teaching out of Hebrews 6:4-6. It reads:

" For it is impossible for those who were once enlightened, and have tasted of the heavenly gift, and were made partakers of the Holy Ghost, And have tasted the good word of God, and the powers of the world to come, If they shall fall away, to renew them again unto repentance; seeing they crucify to themselves *the Son of God afresh, and put him to an open shame"* (emphasis author's).

I admit, the above passage of Scripture is a very challenging one, which, if not interpreted in context, can lead to misinterpretation. Before I address these verses in the book of Hebrews, I want to lay the foundation about basic Bible interpretation, before any kind of scripturally accurate application can be reached. Space limitation in this book prevents me from delving into the topic of Bible exegesis (i.e., to critically examine a Bible text or Scripture in regards to its original intended meaning) and hermeneutics (i.e., to simply apply the Bible text or Scripture in the "here and now", that is to say, to simply understand how the Bible text applies to us, today). Nonetheless, before I can address Hebrews 6:4-6, some basic principles of Bible interpretation is crucial, so I discuss some of these very briefly below:

> Firstly, it is best to ask some basic questions about the Bible text of interest. Such as but not limited to: *(a) Why the book of the Bible was written? (b) Who were the original audience? (c) What circumstances led to the author writing the particular book of the Bible? (d) What message was God telling the audience at the time the book was written?*

> Secondly, there is a simple, straight forward and general rule in interpreting Scripture, that we should never take a Scripture out of context. Rather, to get a fuller understanding of any Scripture, you should read a couple of chapters, or at the very least, a couple of verses, before and after the verse or chapter of the Bible you are interested in, that way you would get a contextual understanding of what the Scripture is teaching.

> Thirdly, you should also look at other books of the Bible, in relation to the verse, chapter of interest, or topic; that is to say, you should examine the totality of All Scriptures in regards to the topic, verse or chapter of interest.

➢ Fourthly, you should then ask basic questions such as this: *What does other books of the Bible say about the particular topic I am interested in?* It is a very bad Bible interpretation habit to take a verse, chapter or even an entire book of the Bible out of context; this practice will definitely lead to heresy (i.e., false teaching).

➢ Fifthly, after considering who the audience was when the book of the Bible was written, and you have evaluated the circumstances surrounding why the book was written, ask yourself questions such as: *How does this issue/topic pertain to me today? What is the Lord teaching me here? And how can I apply this principle/ lesson from the Scripture into my life practically, today?* If we want to be honest with a topic, verse or chapter in the Bible, we must carry out this simple exercise, as discussed above, in order to prevent us from making incorrect interpretations and assumptions about a biblical text or principle.

Application

With the above said, it is relevant to understand that the writer of the book of Hebrews was writing to Jews (i.e., **the audience**), who were brand new Christians, and he was warning them about the dangers of apostasy (i.e., falling away from Christianity and returning to Judaism which was and is still hopeless). These brand new Hebrew Christians were very young as Christians and thus, were possibly struggling with their faith in Christ, and were probably considering returning to Judaism (i.e., **the circumstances**). Given their circumstances, the writer of the book of Hebrews was warning them that if they abandon Christianity and return to Judaism, they would cut themselves off of God's forgiveness found in Christ, because there is no forgiveness apart from Christ (i.e., **the absolute Truth/the principle**). Thus, anyone who cuts Christ off will never receive His salvation, because Christ has already died once, He will never die again, the Hebrews writer insisted.

Church history tells us that during the era when the book of Hebrews was written, it was highly probable that some of these Jews were actually not true followers of the Lord (i.e., **application, the writer of the book of Hebrews was likely not writing to genuine Christians**). In essence, some of them were probably "trying" out Christianity, and were contemplating to return to Judaism; hence, the writer warned them sternly not to do that, because if they allowed their hearts to become callused to the extent of blasphemy (i.e., the unpardonable sin, meaning a willful rejection of Christ as Lord and Savior), there would be no grace or forgiveness for them through Christ (i.e., **application, in regards to those who reject Christ**).

In context, it appears that the writer of the book of Hebrews was not even addressing genuine born again

Christians when he penned his warning as stated out of Hebrews 6:4-6. So, with the above thought: **Are you a genuine follower of Christ?** If yes, then, this warning in this passage of Scripture does not apply to you. On the other hand, if you are a counterfeit, then, this passage of Scripture is speaking directly to you! So evaluate yourself, right now; God already knows your heart, so the best thing is to be honest about your relationship with Him!

Some Bible teachers have interpreted Hebrews 6:4-6 to imply that it refers to true believers who have "fallen away" after becoming "enlightened" with God's Truths and have operated in the gifts of the Spirit, because unbelievers could not be "enlightened" nor be able to taste the "heavenly gifts". Well, I disagree with this interpretation. You know why? Because there are unbelievers who have an outward appearance of godliness , and they have fellowshipped and "hung around" Christians long enough to understand the "Christianee language", such as "Praise the Lord"; "Hallelujah"; "Glory to God", etc, and they might even use some of these phraseologies in their daily dialogues, but that does not make them a true convert—Only time can tell. **Attending church and various Christian activities does not make a person a genuine follower of Jesus Christ, the person must be born again, genuinely from his or her heart, without being coerced.**

Additionally, if a person is not a true convert in the first place, eventually his or her superficiality will be exposed as they would "fall away". But remember, the person would "fall away" because he or she was not genuine in the first place. A classic example of this in the Bible is Judas Iscariot, who was with God Himself for about three years. Judas Iscariot had all of the outward evidence of a true follower of Christ, but time revealed his true identity - he was a counterfeit!

Most importantly, just a basic study of All of the Scriptures pertaining to your salvation will reveal that a true genuine follower of Christ cannot lose his or her salvation. God is consistent, so is His Word. Thus, using one Scripture in the Bible to insist that a person could lose his or her salvation in Christ is not a fair, honest and/or genuine method to interpret God's Word.

So based on the above brief arguments from the Holy Scripture, I hope you are in agreement that, if you have genuinely placed your faith in Jesus Christ as your personal Lord and Savior, your salvation is secured. Again: No, you cannot lose a genuine salvation in Christ, so relax!

If you are concerned about your salvation, instead of worrying about it, simply acknowledge and confess your sins before God, accept His free gift of salvation, and settle the matter once and for all right now! Do that by inviting Jesus Christ into your life as your personal Lord and Savior, and start experiencing peace with God today!

....

WHAT HAPPENS IF I REJECT JESUS CHRIST AS THE MESSIAH?

Question # 14: What Happens if I reject Jesus Christ as the Messiah?

Answer: I hope you do not make that wrong decision. But if you reject Jesus Christ as the Messiah, your personal Lord and Savior , and as The Only way to the True living God and you die, the Bible teaches that you will go straight to hell (i.e., separation from God in all eternity).

The Lord Jesus warned that blasphemy is the only unpardonable sin. In the context (see Matthew 12:32) , the Lord Jesus was teaching that a blasphemous act would be a willful denial or rejection of the presence and power of God's work , and instead, calling it Satanic. Thus, those who , by their own choice, refuse to accept God's work of salvation on the cross, and vehemently reject the convictions of the Holy Spirit will go to hell if they die, because rejecting the conviction of the Holy Spirit is the only unforgivable sin by God.

The Bible teaches us that God takes no pleasure in the suffering of the wicked, or in those who commit blasphemy

(Ezekiel 33:11); but rather, He wants the wicked to repent and live. Also, God is patient and long suffering, wanting no one to go to hell, but for everyone to repent and to accept His free gift to mankind— Jesus Christ (2 Peter 3:9;1 Timothy 2: 4). Hell was created for Satan and his angels, and not for human beings (Matthew 25:41); so it is not God's wish for anyone to go to this horrible place, but people willingly choose to go there.

It is very critical that I explain the fact that God is love, in His very nature (1 John 4:8), and He does not send anyone to hell. In fact, God has provided a way for people not to go to hell: Jesus Christ.

And in His love and patience, God is giving people unlimited amount of chances to repent, and He is endlessly placing "barriers" in their paths, preventing them from going to hell. He does this by sending His co-workers into people's paths to proclaim the Gospel, and the Holy Spirit is continuously convicting people to come to repentance; yet, countless numbers of people are still rejecting God's free gift: Jesus Christ, and are sending themselves to hell. It is very scary that the book of Revelation teaches that in the last days, people will be given several opportunities to repent from their wickedness, and in spite of their obvious suffering, they will still blaspheme God and refuse to accept Jesus Christ (see Revelation chapter 16).

This goes to show you that it is an issue of the heart: pride! But this is not God's will for anyone.

Another misconception about hell is that only criminals and evil people go there, while "good" people go to heaven after death. This is so unscriptural and wrong. Hell and heaven have nothing to do with your " good actions" per say—it is not about being good or bad in this life. <u>Rather, the determining factor whether or not a person ends up in hell or heaven is the decision he or she makes about Jesus Christ, period!</u>

Heaven is filled with criminals and all sorts of "bad" people, but they made the right decision to accept Jesus Christ as their personal Lord and Savior. And while still on this earth, the process of sanctification started (i.e., God started to change them into the image of Christ), and when they die, they will be fully conformed to the image of Christ in heaven.

On the other hand, hell is filled with very "good" and "morally upright and self-righteous" people, who committed blasphemy, and rejected Jesus Christ as their personal Lord and Savior, and

were deceived into thinking that their good moral "works" would gain them an entrance into heaven: NO, it cannot, you can only get to heaven through Jesus Christ, period!

And unfortunately, there are those who have totally rejected the entire doctrine of hell as taught in the Bible, and have refused that hell is a real place. In fact, the Lord Jesus Himself, God in the flesh, taught very much about hell (e g., Matthew 8:12; 13: 49-50; Luke 12:5), as a real place. Hell is also described in the Bible as a "lake of fire" and a "place of darkness" (Matthew 11:20-24; 13: 49-50 ; 2 Peter 2:4), with "everlasting suffering and torture".

Much worse, those in hell will have full consciousness about their suffering (Luke 16:19-31). My intention is not to scare you, but to tell you the truth, because "fear tactics" will not produce any lasting change in your heart. Rather, it is the love and goodness of God that leads to a true heartfelt repentance (Romans 2:4).

So if you have been depending on your "good works" or some other way to take you to heaven, today is the day for you to repent, and accept Jesus Christ as your personal Lord and Savior, right now. If you have been reading this book thus far, you know exactly what to do and how to make that decision, so proceed and act in faith, right now, and ask Jesus Christ into your life, then you will not go to hell once you die! Death is imminent, it is the all time "equalizer"— everyone dies, sooner or later! But, do you know where you are going after you die? You want to be certain you know today, right now!

Hopefully you have accepted Jesus Christ as your personal Lord and Savior. If yes, then, you do not need to be afraid of dying, because Jesus overcame death. He is alive today! And you will be alive with Him as well upon your death and transition into eternity! Hallelujah!

....

DID JESUS CHRIST COME TO THE EARTH TO START A RELIGION CALLED CHRISTIANITY?

Question # 15: Did Jesus Christ come to the Earth to Start a Religion Called Christianity?

Answer: No, He did not! He came primarily as the Son of God, the promised Messiah, in order to proclaim the Kingdom of God, and to reveal the true nature of God the Father, to us, Mankind.

The main goal of Jesus Christ was not to begin a religious movement called Christianity, as some critics have charged; rather, He came to preach about the "Kingdom of God" and to redeem Mankind from the bondage of sin, and to overcome Satan. But true Christianity originated from the teachings, beliefs and practices of Jesus Christ of Nazareth, as such, He is considered to be the founder of the faith. As part of this question, it is necessary that I define some terminologies associated with the word Christianity, thus enhancing clarity.

WHO IS THE REAL JESUS?

The word Christian, is an English translation from the Greek word *"Christianos"* meaning "follower of Christ," or *"adherent of Jesus."* The word "Christ" comes from the Greek word *"Christos,"* which means *"anointed,"* and is translated as *"Messiah,"* a title of Jesus of Nazareth: - *The Christ*; our Lord Jesus accepted this title during His earthly ministry (Matthew 16: 16-17; John 4:26; Mark 14:61-62).

Following the death, burial and resurrection of Jesus Christ, His followers or adherents during the first Century did not call themselves Christians, the Gentiles (i.e., all non-Jewish individuals) did, and it was in Antioch that the followers of Jesus were first called Christians (Acts 11:26). Then, at some point during the first Century, the word Christians, as used by the Gentiles, had an implication of scorn and persecution. In First Peter 4:16, the apostle Peter recognized and accepted the name on the basis of persecution.

And during the apostle Paul's defense of the Gospel in Acts chapter 26, King Agrippa used the word Christian (v.28), in recognition that accepting the apostle Paul's defense would make him a Christian (v. 28). By this point, the word Christianity was well known among the Gentiles. And moving forward till the present time, the word Christianity has been associated with a *"follower of Christ"* or " *adherent of Jesus,"* and with persecution.

So NO, Jesus Christ's primary focus was to fulfill His role as the Messiah, and to reveal God the Father, and His kingdom to us.

He is the Messiah! Have you accepted Him into your heart by faith? Jesus Christ revealed the true living God to the world: His love, compassion, forgiveness, grace, justice, etc. Do you not want to know this compassionate and loving God? I am sure you would say yes; if that is so, have you accepted Him into your life? If not, go ahead and invite Jesus Christ into your life today, and start walking in His peace, joy, protection, etc, and discover your real purpose in this life.

....

Did Jesus Christ Teach about Heaven?

Question # 16: Did Jesus Christ Teach about Heaven?

Answer: Yes, He did.

The Bible teaches that heaven is a real physical place (John 14:2), created by God (Genesis 1:1), where The eternal God dwells; it is not an ideology like some people believe. Jesus Christ Himself came from heaven, and after His death and resurrection, He ascended back into heaven (John 3:13; 14:1-3), where He is now seated at the right hand of God the Father (Colossians 3:1-3).

The Lord Jesus did not teach a lot about heaven like most of us would have liked. But He called it a "paradise" (Luke 23:43), a place of "everlasting security and safety" (Matthew 6:19-21; Luke 12:33), and a place where those "who love God will worship Him forevermore" (see Revelation Chapter 4), and "spend eternity" with Him (John 10:28).

In His teaching about heaven, the Lord Jesus taught that there are many individuals who call upon Him, but they are counterfeits, meaning they are not His true followers (Matthew 13: 24-30). The Lord then warned that in spite of all the millions of people calling upon His name and claiming to love Him, only a few of them (that is to say, His true followers) will enter through the narrow gate leading into heaven (Matthew 7:13-14), and the counterfeits will end up in hell (Matthew 25:31-46).

With regards to counterfeit followers of Christ Jesus , here is His stern warning to them:

"Not everyone who calls out to me, 'Lord! Lord!' will enter the Kingdom of Heaven. Only those who actually do the will of my Father in heaven will enter. On judgment day many will say to me, 'Lord! Lord! We prophesied in your name and cast out demons in your name and performed many miracles in your name.' But I will reply, 'I never knew you. Get away from me, you who break God's laws.'..." (Matthew 7:21-27).

Heaven is a Real Place

There is an unfathomable future in heaven for all those who love God (1 Corinthians 2:9; 2 Corinthians 12:4). In addition to the brief teachings from our Lord about heaven, the Scriptures have also given us some glimpses about heaven, thus offering much hope to us. For example, the Bible describes heaven as a place where all of our suffering will end; heaven has streets made of pure gold (see Revelation chapter 21); the glory of God will illuminate heaven, so that there will be no night there nor need for the sun or light to light it up (Revelation 22: 1-6).

Much more, the Bible teaches that we will recognize and know each other in heaven (1 Corinthians 13:12), and there will be a great reunion with our loved ones who died as Christians; we will also forget all things pertaining to this present life (Isaiah 65:17). There is also a permanent separation (i.e., fixed division) between heaven and hell, so that no one can cross over to the other side (Luke 16:19-30). Additionally, heaven is a place of perfection (1 Peter 1:4); we will be given new glorified bodies, just like the resurrected body of our Lord Jesus Christ (1 Corinthians 15:51-52). And, we will, finally, see Jesus Christ, our Lord and Savior, our God, face to face! Hallelujah, let us praise the Lord! (1 John 3:2; Revelation 22:4).

Just the brief discussion above about heaven gives me "goose bumps"!

For the true Christian, heaven is indeed the blessed hope we have in Christ Jesus, by faith! This is real, because God says so, period, whether or not you believe it.

But I hope you do! So let me ask you a question: Do you know beyond a shadow of doubt, in your heart, that when you die, you will go to heaven? If not, you can change that today, right now.

If you want to change your destination from hell to heaven after death, you can do that right now, by simply asking Jesus Christ to become your personal Lord and Savior. If you believe in your heart that Jesus died for your sins and was raised from the dead on the third day, and you desire to become His true follower, simply ask Him to come into your life right now, and He will. If you need help doing this, go back to chapter 1 of this book, and simply say out loud that simple prayer.

CHAPTER 17

IS JESUS CHRIST REALLY COMING BACK TO THE EARTH?

Question # 17: Is Jesus Christ Really Coming Back to the Earth?

Answer: Yes, He is!

For those of you who might be thinking that the answer to this question is obvious, it is really not so for many people, who are erroneously believing that Jesus Christ already came, and/or that He will not return physically to this earth. Many people believe this lie from the pit of hell, from Satan himself. Indeed, Christ Jesus is definitely coming back in bodily form, just like He ascended into heaven after His resurrection, and He will return in a way that everyone will see Him (Acts 1:11). Below are just a few Scriptures that are very clear that Jesus Christ will return:

➢ **Matthew 24:30**:

"Then will appear the sign of the Son of Man in heaven. And then all the peoples of the earth will mourn when they see the

Son of Man coming on the clouds of heaven, with power and great glory...."

> ➤ **John 14:3**:

" *And if I go and prepare a place for you, I will come back and take you to be with me that you also may be where I am."*

> ➤ **Revelation 1:7**:

"Look, he is coming with the clouds," and "every eye will see him, even those who pierced him"; and all peoples on earth "will mourn because of him." So shall it be! Amen."

1 Thessalonians 4:16:

"For the Lord himself will come down from heaven, with a loud command, with the voice of the archangel and with the trumpet call of God, and the dead in Christ will rise first."

Acts 1:11:

"Men of Galilee," they said, "why do you stand here looking into the sky? This same Jesus, who has been taken from you into heaven, will come back in the same way you have seen him go into heaven."

As you can see from the Scriptures above, our Lord will definitely be returning, and He gave us specific signs to watch for, that must be fulfilled before He returns to the earth. In what is popularly called the Olivet Discourse, out of the Gospel of Matthew chapter 24, Christ Jesus discussed, on the Mount of Olives, specific signs for us to watch for, before His return. Since the focus of this book or chapter is not on end times, I will not dwell much into this topic; but for clarity, and to answer the question about the second coming of Christ, it is relevant that I discuss some of the basic signs, taught by the Lord Himself, for us to watch for, as clues before His final return to the earth. Below I discuss some of these signs briefly:

The Lord said before His return, the following must happen, as stated in Matthew chapter 24:

1. **Many antichrists will come**. He said *"For many will come in my name, claiming, 'I am the* Messiah,' and will deceive many"* (v. 5);

2. **The world will experience continuous wars**. He said: *" You will hear of wars and rumors of wars, but see to it that you are not alarmed. Such things must happen, but the end is still to come"* (v. 6);

3. **There will be fighting against the nations of the earth**. *The Lord noted: "Nation will rise against nation, and kingdom against kingdom"* (v. 7);

4. **There will be earthquakes and famine across the world.** Christ said *" There will be famines and*

earthquakes in various places. All these are the beginning of birth pains" (v. 7);

5. **There will be severe persecution in the body of Christ** (i.e., all true Christians across the world regardless of denominational preference, gender or nationality will suffer severe persecution), and many will hate Him. Jesus explained " *Then you will be handed over to be persecuted and put to death, and you will be hated by all nations because of me"* (v.9);

6. **False teaching and lawlessness will abound** (i.e., overt sin against God and His holy standards) will proliferate and many will deny God. He explained: *"At that time many will turn away from the faith and will betray and hate each other, and many false prophets will appear and deceive many people. Because of the increase of wickedness, the love of most will grow cold"* (vv. 10-12);

7. **The Gospel must be proclaimed to all the nations**, He explained *"And this gospel of the kingdom will be preached in the whole world as a testimony to all nations, and then the end will come"* (v. 14).

Still in Matthew chapter 24, the Lord went on to describe how He will appear in a visible way for all to see.

And He warned that when we see the above signs, we should take heed that the time of His return to the earth is imminent (vv. 30-35).

It is interesting that in the last many Centuries and years, many people have attempted to predict when Christ Jesus will return. But unfortunately, all such predictions will only lead to a dead end, because no one truly knows.

But Jesus Christ Himself Did Not Know the Time of His Second Return, Right?

This mystery about the exact return of Jesus Christ has led many people to question the Lord's Deity as God, because He said: *"But about that day or hour no one knows, not even the angels in heaven, nor the Son, but only the Father"* (Matthew 24:36).

The fact that the Lord Jesus said when He was on the earth, that He did not know the exact hour of His coming does not nullify His deity.

You know why? Because as already described in the preceding chapters, the Lord Jesus Christ was 100% man and 100% God.

As a man, Jesus Christ operated and performed miracles under the power of the Holy Spirit, and was 100% dependent on God the Father. In His human nature therefore, Christ Jesus chose to humble Himself, and was submissive to God the Father, and was in 100% cooperation with His limitations of being a human being (Philippians 2:7).

Thus, by His own choice, due to His humility and obedience to God the Father, He chose to limit Himself to the exact and/or precise knowledge about His second coming, thus He stated He did not know the time of His second coming.

But after His resurrection, we can be assured that the Lord Jesus, who knows all things (John 21:17), now knows the exact date, hour, and second of His second coming to the earth. So, now that, we, as His followers, do not know the exact time the Lord is coming, what do we do?

What to Do While Waiting For Christ's Return

Since we do not know when our Lord and Savior will return, we have to continue living, and be acutely vigilant and be ready for His return (Matthew 25: 1-13). Before His ascension into heaven, the Lord gave us a commandment, commonly called the **Great Commission,** which is to proclaim the Gospel and make disciples (i.e., to teach others) (Matthew 28:19-20). This commandment pertains to each individual Christian, and not just to the Universal Church or professional ministers. Also, the Lord Himself taught us that we should be advancing His Kingdom until He returns (Luke 19:13). So while waiting for His return, continue to witness to others about Christ Jesus; attend church; advance God's Kingdom on the earth by serving in your local church or other ministries; be a good steward of whatever God has blessed you with, such as, but not limited to raising godly children, your finances, your relationships, etc.

I have heard of so many Christians who are not being responsible in their earthly duties, because they are anticipating and expecting Christ's return soon. If you do this, STOP! Right now! Get busy with life, being a good witness for Christ. The worst thing you can do is to give away all of your property and/or possession, and become lazy and careless in hopes that Christ will come in the next few weeks or years —Church history tells us that many Christians have done this! Just like the Lord has told us in the Olivet Discourse, I am reiterating His teaching here—You do not know the day or hour of His return, and do not trust anyone who tells you he or she does, because that would be a lie. Thus, get busy with life and live to glorify Christ in your actions.

All previous generations and centuries have anticipated that Christ will return during their lifetime, and it did not happen. Nonetheless, one thing is certain: His return is imminent, because of various events happening in the world today, all pointing to the perfect setting for Christ's return. For example, in this 21st Century compared to other Centuries, the Gospel Message of Christ is spreading very fast, due in part because of the advancement in technology; English is the dominant language of most countries in the world today, setting the stage for a "common trade" across the globe, which is one of the elements than has to be in place at the time the final antichrist is revealed.

Since Christ gave the famous Olivet Discourse, it has been over 2000 years, thus, so much time has elapsed; this alone makes it probable that His coming is near. Also, a lot of the Jews are migrating back to Jerusalem, fulfilling prophecy and setting the stage for end times, because Jerusalem will play a major role in the end times. Much more, many antichrists have come and gone (1 John 2:18), but the final antichrist has not yet been revealed; because the world is not quite ready for him, although many events are currently happening in the world today in preparation for his rule. Unfortunately, as predicted by Christ Jesus, lawlessness and hatred of God is already rampant today in government, school systems, etc, etc. All of these events are setting the stage for Christ's return, and I am very hopeful, and I want to see Him come today!

For those of you worried about the catastrophic events that must take place before Christ's return, take heart! And put it all in godly perspective. Remember, Jesus said when we see and hear of all these events, we should take them as signs that He is coming. Thus, instead of being fearful and worried that the world is coming to an end; rejoice, because it means that your Lord is coming, very soon. Putting all these "crazy" world events in biblical perspective will engender the peace of God. Most importantly, be vigilant and be ready, Christ might come today! If He does, will you be ready? if not, why not? You can fix that today, right now! Simply ask Him to be your Lord and Savior, then you will be able to relax!

....

WHAT MAKES JESUS CHRIST DIFFERENT?

Question # 18: What Makes Jesus Christ Different?

Answer: He was the Only Son of God; the Messiah, God Himself in the flesh; His miracles were undeniably unmatched. <u>Jesus Christ is The Only One Who is Real</u>!

Firstly, Jesus Christ was not, and is not a religious leader, it is relevant that you know this outright!

I only discuss Him here as a religious leader in context with the so called self proclaimed religious leaders, in order to enhance clarity of the discussion. As you know by now, if you have been reading through this book, Jesus Christ was God Himself in the flesh, God's Only Son, a human being like one of us, and the Messiah of the world. He was the best teacher who ever lived, and He taught God's laws and wisdom with authority (Matthew 7:29), and revealed the character and nature of God the Father to us, His creation (Hebrews 1:1-2).

Although Jesus Christ is a stark contrast to all of the counterfeit world religious leaders such as Muhammad (Islam); Joseph Smith (Mormonism); Confucius (Chinese Religions); Krishna (Hinduism); Charles Russell (Jehovah's Witnesses), etc, this is a critical question because there are many uninformed individuals who believe that our Lord and Savior, was just like one of the hundreds of self-proclaimed world religious leaders. For others, it is a willful denial of the true identity of Jesus Christ, as such, they put Him in the same category as other religious leaders in the world, which is 100% incorrect.

It will take hundreds of pages to expound on why Jesus Christ is in a class of His own, but due to space limitation, I am unable to do so in this chapter. Thus, to answer this question succinctly, I have placed the major differences between Jesus Christ and All other self-proclaimed religious leaders in the following table:

JESUS CHRIST	ALL SELF-PROCLAIMED RELIGIOUS LEADERS
Is Eternal He was not a created being; He has always existed	**Created human beings,** born into this world with a Sinful Nature
Had a Divine birth (i.e., the incarnation, born into this world sinless)	**Experienced a human birth** (i.e., born as a sinner), requiring a Messiah to redeem them
Was The Teacher from God; taught Only what He heard from God the Father; taught original Truths from the Heavenly realm	**Taught/Teaches secondary embellished** truths and philosophies of Man
Expressed the highest degree of unfathomable Unconditional love (i.e., He forgave others, died on the cross for others, etc)	**Expresses conditional love** based on performances, good service/works, etc

JESUS CHRIST	ALL SELF-PROCLAIMED RELIGIOUS LEADERS
Performed undeniable, verifiable and corroborated miracles, unmatched	**No evidence of** such verifiable and corroborated evidence of miracles exists
Prophecies All came to pass with 100% precision	No such evidence exists
Called Himself God and backed it up with 100% verifiable, proven and corroborated evidence	No such evidence exists
Stated unequivocally that (1) He is The Only Way to eternal life; (2) He is the Resurrection; (3) He forgives sins, (4) He is eternal, etc. He backed up these claims with 100% verifiable evidence	No such evidence exists, and will never exist in the history of the world
Was raised from the dead as prophesied, and is alive today, right now	All of these people are still dead. A dead person cannot save anyone

JESUS CHRIST	ALL SELF-PROCLAIMED RELIGIOUS LEADERS
Is Omniscient (knows All things); Omnipotent (all powerful), Omnipresent (is everywhere)	Limited in knowledge, power and presence, because they are mere human beings
The Only way to The Only True living God of the Bible	No such claim exists. Depending on "good works" to enter heaven, which is impossible, Jesus Christ is The Only ticket to heaven
Fulfilled All of God's perfect Laws 100%	No such claim exists
Desires a **heartfelt relationship** with His followers, which is liberating and freeing, leading to much peace, true happiness, joy and, an **abundant life**	Desires religion, a do's and don'ts type of relationship which leads to fear, anxiety, bondage, death and a **dead end**
Guarantees eternity with God upon death, to His followers; etc; etc;.	No promise of eternity exists.

The list is endless, but I am certain you get the obvious point. You cannot even begin to compare Jesus Christ with the self-proclaimed religious leaders of the world: It is like night and day. All world religious leaders are sinners, needing Jesus Christ to save them from their Sinful Fallen states as human beings. Do not allow Satan to deceive you anymore: Jesus Christ is The Only Way to God!

As described above, none of them claimed to be God and backed it up with 100% verifiable and corroborated evidence, except Jesus Christ, the perfect lamb of God, who is still alive today, desiring a heartfelt relationship with you. Are you ready for such a relationship? Do you personally know Jesus Christ? If not, and you have been reading this book thus far, you know exactly what to do, so proceed and ask Him into your life right now, and He will accept.

....

IS CHRIST JESUS MENTIONED IN THE OLD TESTAMENT?

Question # 19: Is Christ Jesus Mentioned in the Old Testament?

Answer: Yes, in His Pre-Incarnate form, meaning, before He became a human being.

The Bible teaches us, as I have already explained in the preceding chapters that Jesus Christ, the second person of the Godhead, has always existed. And yes, He manifested, in His Pre-incarnate form throughout the Old Testament era, and then in His incarnate form (i.e., as a human being) in the New Testament (John 1:1-14).

In studying the doctrine of Christology (meaning the study of Christ), specifically the Pre-Incarnate Christ, Bible scholars generally agree that various Old Testament texts that mention "The Angel of the Lord", are indeed appearances of Christ Jesus Himself in His Pre-incarnate form, especially in those appearances when the "The Angel of the Lord" accepted worship. You may wonder why? It is noteworthy to remember that in the Old Testament, angels appeared to various individuals; however, the difference is that, when "The Angel of the Lord" appeared to various individuals, He was called God and accepted to be worshipped: this was the major difference.

Much more, "The Angel of the Lord" did not rebuke the worshipper who worshipped Him, when He appeared to the person.

This is significant because God has clearly told us in His Word to flee from idolatry, and that only Him is to be worshipped (e.g., Exodus 34:14; Luke 4:8), because He is our Creator.

As such, even though angels are supernatural beings, they are created beings who are not to be worshipped. And often, in the Scriptures, angels would refuse to be worshipped when they appear to individuals (e.g., Revelation 22:8-9).

Appearances of the Pre Incarnate Christ in the Old Testament

Because "The Angel of the Lord" is different from ordinary angels, it is generally accepted, as you will learn from the Scriptures below, that His appearances were indeed those of the Pre - incarnate Christ Himself. Also, keep in mind that in these appearances of "The Angel of the Lord", those individuals who saw "The Angel of the Lord" stated that they had seen God, and in fact worshipped Him. There are too many appearances for me to list all of them. Below are just a few:

❖ *Genesis 32:24-30:*

> *So Jacob was left alone, and a man wrestled with him till daybreak. When the man saw that he could not overpower him, he touched the socket of Jacob's hip so that his hip was wrenched as he wrestled with the man.... "Your name will no longer be Jacob, but Israel, because you have struggled with God and with humans and have overcome." Jacob said, "Please tell me your name."But he replied, "Why do you ask my name?" Then he blessed him there. So Jacob called the place Peniel, saying, "It is because I saw God face to face, and yet my life was spared" (vv. 24-30).*

❖ **Genesis 16:7-15**:

> *The angel of the Lord found Hagar near a spring in the desert; it was the spring that is beside the road to Shur.... She gave this name to the Lord who spoke to her: "You are the God who sees me," for she said, "I have now seen the One who sees me." That is why the well was called Beer Lahai Roi ; it is still there, between Kadesh and Bered. So Hagar bore Abram a son, and Abram gave the name Ishmael to the son she had borne (vv. 7-15).*

❖ **Judges 6:11-14**:

*The angel of the Lord came and sat down under the oak in Ophrah that belonged to Joash the Abiezrite, where his son Gideon was threshing wheat in a winepress to keep it from the Midianites....**The Lord turned to him and said**, "Go in the strength you have and save Israel out of Midian's hand. Am I not sending you?" (vv. 11-14).*

❖ **Hosea 12: 3-5**

*In the womb he grasped his brother's heel; as a man he struggled with God. He struggled with the angel and overcame him; he wept and begged for his favor. He found him at Bethel and talked with him there— **the Lord God Almighty, the Lord is his name!** (vv. 3-5).*

❖ **Judges 6:20-24**:

*Then the angel of the Lord touched the meat and the unleavened bread with the tip of the staff that was in his hand. Fire flared from the rock, consuming the meat and the bread. And the angel of the Lord disappeared... When Gideon realized that it was the angel of the Lord, he exclaimed, "**Alas, Sovereign Lord! I have seen the angel of the Lord face to face!**" But the Lord said to him, "Peace! Do not be afraid. You are not going to die." So Gideon built an altar to the Lord there and called it The Lord Is Peace. To this day it stands in*

Ophrah of the Abiezrites (vv.20-24).

Other Scriptures of the appearances of the Pre-incarnate Christ include but are not limited to Zechariah 12:8; 2 Kings 19:35; Daniel 3:10-28; 2 Samuel 14:17-20 etc, etc, etc.

Then the incarnate Christ Jesus Himself attested to His appearances in the Old Testament. One such example is documented in the Gospel of John 8:57-58, when the Lord Jesus told the Pharisees that before Abraham was "I am", alluding to His presence in the burning bush experience as recorded in Exodus chapter 3.

Recall that in Exodus chapter 3, "The Angel of the Lord" (i.e., the Pre Incarnate Christ Himself) appeared to Moses in the burning bush (v.2). Then, "The Angel of the Lord" said to Moses: *"I am the God of your father, the God of Abraham, the God of Isaac and the God of Jacob." At this, Moses hid his face, because he was afraid to look at God "* (v.6). As you can see from this Scripture, it was Jesus Christ Himself, as He confirmed it in the Gospels, who appeared to Moses in His pre-incarnate form.

I once told someone that if they were to take away the New Testament from the entire Bible, I will still be able to preach and teach about Jesus Christ (Pre-incarnate) based on the Old Testament writings. I hope you can agree with my statement. Yes indeed, Christ Jesus Himself, in His pre-incarnate form appeared throughout the Old Testament era to people, and He was present in the creation of the universe — Jesus has always existed; He is eternal, and will always exist, because He is God Himself.

Do you know this Jesus? If no, He wants you to know Him personally today. If you are ready, genuinely invite Him into your life by faith, and He will come in, and your life will never be the same.

DID JESUS TEACH ABOUT MONEY?

Question # 20: Did Jesus Teach About Money?

Answer: Yes, He did.

Some of you may wonder why this question is relevant, but you would be amazed by the number of people who are unaware that our Lord taught about money, and offered timeless Truths and principles on how to manage our finances. The issue of money and the Church is so involved that, I will only focus on the key principles taught by the Lord about money in this brief chapter.

Before I even begin, I must emphasize that, if you are a true Christian, you should understand a major principle about your wealth, as taught in the Bible. It is the absolute Truth that God owns everything you possess, including All of your money and other possessions. Your role is to become a good steward of whatever God has blessed you with, because He is the one who enabled you to obtain the wealth and all of your possessions in the first place (Deuteronomy 8:18). So, please, change your perspective about your so called "wealth."

Then, there are individuals, who unfortunately, have the attitude that they have worked for everything they own; and as such, no one should tell them how to use their money or possession; this is a very ungodly attitude.

> **While it is true that you might have worked hard for your wealth, remember that it is God, who gave you the strength and/or ability to work hard. So at the end of the day, the major principle from God's Word is that — you are just managing what belongs to God in the first place.**

With this main principle in mind, be aware that All of the Lord's teachings about money will center around this principle. Below are the principles:

➢ **Matthew 17:24-27**

The Lord Jesus taught that we should pay taxes, period! He exemplified this by paying taxes Himself, which showed respect for the government establishment.

➢ **Luke 10:29-37**

The Lord taught that we should use our money and financial resources to assist those in need, and the poor. By helping the poor, the Lord is not implying that we should strip ourselves of all wealth, and become poor ourselves in order to assist others: No. This is a very wrong doctrine that many are upholding, that Christians are to strip themselves of all earthly wealth, because the Lord made a comment to a "certain rich man" who came to inquire of Him, as to how he could be His follower. Here was the Lord's response : *"You still lack one thing. Sell everything you have and give to the poor, and you will have treasure in heaven. Then* come, *follow me"* (Luke18:18-25), (emphasis author's).

If you were to study the totality of the teachings in the Scriptures, it would become obvious that the Lord's comment to this "certain man" was primarily highlighting a major principle: which is the fact that money cannot provide the type of lasting security and peace human beings desire. Also, this "certain man" was focusing on his "good works", claiming he had done everything in the Law, rather than coming to Christ as a sinner, in need of a Savior. It is my belief that Christ asked this "certain man" to sell all of his possessions before becoming His follower, because He knew that this man was believing more in his wealth, than in the true living God. Remember, the Lord knows all things, it could also be possible that this was a test for this man who claimed He wanted to be a follower of the Lord, but the Lord knew that he was not sincere, thus He tested Him, asking him to sell all of his possessions.

Furthermore, the Lord probably discerned that this man's wealth was his "god", thus He tested him, just to reveal his true intentions. And obviously, this young man walked away, after hearing the Lord's request, thus confirming that he really was not ready to "give up" his carnal appetites and his "god", and become a true follower of the Lord (see Luke 18:18-25). **This story in the Bible is by no means prescriptive, meaning, the Lord is not implying or teaching that All of His followers should sell their possessions in order to follow Him: No!**

Luke 10:1-9

Christ taught that we should use our money to support His work on the earth, financially supporting genuine missionaries, ministers, teachers and pastors, who are truthfully proclaiming the Gospel and teaching God's Word.

> ## Mark 12:41-44

The Lord supported the notion of us giving our offerings to the churches and similar Christ centered events and activities that foster His Kingdom here on the earth. Another major principle the Lord taught in these Scriptures (**Mark 12:41-44**) is the fact that God is not necessarily after how much we give; rather, He is after our sacrificial giving in faith, out of what we have. Additionally, here is the other principle out of the Scripture:

> **God is very interested in our finances, and how we give, in faith, towards His work: He is watching very closely**.

Here is the Lord's comment about the woman who gave out of her poverty.

Jesus sat down opposite the place where the offerings were put and watched the crowd putting their money into the temple treasury. Many rich people threw in large amounts. But a poor widow came and put in two very small copper coins, worth only a few cents. Calling his disciples to him, Jesus said, "Truly I tell you, this poor widow has put more into the treasury than all the others. They all gave out of their wealth; but she, out of her poverty, put in everything—all she had to live on" (Mark 12: 41-44), (emphasis author's).

In my opinion, this principle is very clear, but I will use an example to illustrate further. As an example, a person may give, say, $50,000 (Fifty thousand dollars, USD), because he or she has 2 (Two) million or more dollars in the bank. But someone else may only give, say, $75 (Seventy- five dollars, USD), because this individual only has $ 100 (One hundred dollars or less , USD) in the bank. Even though God appreciates both of them who would have given in faith; however, in His perspective, the person who gave that $75 dollars, would have given sacrificially, because he or she would have given out of his or her limited amount. So, do not be bothered by how much someone else is giving. Instead, you just give in faith, as you have it , and know for sure that God is watching, just like He was watching at the Temple over 2000 years ago.

> ## Luke 8:1-3

The Lord accepted and collected money from His followers who supported His work. Thus, setting a precedence that truthful ministries, churches and other Christ-centered institutions should accept and collect donations from others, in order to advance God's work here on the earth.

There is a lot I could say about money, but suffice it to say that, God does not need your money. Instead, He wants you to trust Him with your finances, **because He knows that the love of money can wreak havoc in your life** (1 Timothy 6:10), and He is aware that if you trust your money more than Him, your heart will be drawn away from Him as your sole provider and main source for security. Instead, He wants you to invest your money in His Kingdom, in heavenly things which are imperishable (Matthew 6:21). And most importantly, money cannot, and will never provide you with the security and eternal satisfaction that only comes from a solid relationship with God through Christ.

And most significantly, to God, money is a trust issue, because if you can trust Him with your money, which is a tangible object, then it will be much easier for you to trust Him with other things such as healing of physical diseases, restoration of broken relationships, emotional healings, etc. Unfortunately, it has been my experience in ministry that those who struggle the most with trusting God with their problems, are also those who are experiencing major difficulties in trusting God with their money.

If you are struggling with trusting and allowing God to manage your money (i.e., applying biblical principles in managing your money), I recommend that you sincerely work in this area of your life. God has to work through people who are willing to obey Him, so that they can give financially to support His work on the earth. It is His will for you to give towards His work, so trust Him with your money. And there is a general principle that if you give towards God's work, whether financially or through providing good service for the Lord, He will bless you in return, guaranteed: Here is how the Lord Jesus said it: " *Give, and you will receive. Your gift will return to you in full—pressed down, shaken together to make room for more, running over, and poured into your lap. The amount you give will determine the amount you get back"* (Luke 6:38; New Living Translation), (emphasis author's).

You can never out give God; whatever you give, you will in turn receive, exactly as given, and even more!

In addition, giving is a great way for your faith to be strengthened, which will in turn benefit you in all other areas in your life, and solidify your relationship with God. So go ahead and give, trusting God with the outcome, you will be pleased! For God is faithful to His promises; you will be amazed how He will bless you back!

God has already given you the best gift, His Only Son, Jesus Christ – Do you have a relationship with Him? If not, you can change that right this moment by asking Him to come and dwell in your heart by faith, and He will do so, right now!

....

IF JESUS WAS PHYSICALLY ON THE EARTH TODAY, HOW WOULD HE DEAL WITH SIN?

Question # 21: If Jesus was on the Earth today, How would He Deal with Sin?

Answer: The same way He dealt with sin when He was on the earth over 2000 years ago.

By definition, sin is any offence a person commits knowingly or unknowingly, that violates God's perfect laws of holiness and/or perfection. God has Only one standard for comparison: Jesus Christ, the perfect, sinless, Son of God, who fulfilled His holy standards 100%.

I believe that most human beings are aware when they sin against God. Examples of often ignored sins include, but are not limited to: unforgiveness, gossiping, malicious thinking patterns towards others, jealousy, envy, "bad mouthing" others, refusing to assist someone who is in need (especially when you are able to do so), pride, etc. Other obvious sins include, but are not limited to: stealing, cheating, lying, greed, murder, adultery, any sexual relationships outside of marriage, homosexuality, disrespect towards authorities and your parents, rejecting God's gift to Mankind, Jesus Christ, as your personal Lord and Savior, etc, etc. The list of sins against God is endless.

Regardless of the type of sin committed, if the Lord Jesus was still on this earth, He would treat the sinner exactly as He did when He lived on this earth. You know why? Because the Bible teaches us that Christ Jesus is the same yesterday, today, and forevermore — He has not changed in His approach towards people (Hebrews 13:8). So how did He treat the sinner?:

- ✓ He expressed His unconditional love towards the sinner, yet denounced the sinful act (John 8:1-11);

- ✓ He expressed a holy anger towards hypocrites and self-righteous individuals , that is to say, those who were trusting in their own holiness or good works to earn them a good standing with God (Matthew chapter 23; John 2:13-17). And His attitude towards self-righteous individuals is still the same, today;

- ✓ He forgave those who sought for His forgiveness in true repentance (Luke 7:48-49; Matthew 9:1-3) ;

- ✓ He called sin, sin, period! He did not camouflage it; He was direct, and straight to the point, yet humble and loving (John 4:1-26; Matthew chapter 23).

Jesus Christ Is the Same

Since Jesus Christ is the same yesterday, today and

forevermore (Hebrews 13:8), He will definitely treat the sinner in exactly the same way He did as revealed in the Scripture.

Unfortunately, many people are deceived into thinking that the writings in the Bible are ancient and/or archaic ; and thus, they believe that if Jesus Christ was living on the earth today, He would treat sinners differently —NO, this is not true, it is a lie from the devil.

Others are even going as far as saying that since we now live in the 21st Century, God is progressive and as such, He will treat people differently, in accordance with the morals and standards of this Century— again, another lie from Satan, the Master deceiver. God is immutable (i.e., unchangeable) in His core attributes (Numbers 23:19; Malachi 3:6; Hebrews 13:8; James 1:17) . Thus, He still hates sin, has compassion and love for the sinner, wanting the person to repent; and He is ever present and willing to accept a true heartfelt repentance (2 Peter 3:9).

Thus, if Jesus was on the earth today, He would denounce all the various perverse sexual relations happening today such as, but not limited to homosexuality, lesbianism, sex before marriage, incest, and other sins such as lying, gossiping, giving false witness, pride, and **ALL** other perverse and current types of sins. And keep in mind that with God, sin is sin, period! There are no little sins or big sins in God's perspective: sin is sin, period!

So, if you are a Christian who is practicing sin, and being deceived that you are hurting no one; well, firstly, I recommend that you evaluate yourself, if you are a true follower of the Lord Jesus (2 Corinthians 13:5). Secondly, if you are a true Christian, you are primarily hurting God, because all sin is against God primarily, then against yourself and others. So I recommend that you repent and ask the Lord Jesus to cleanse you, and restore you back into fellowship with God the Father (1 John 1:9; 1 John 2:1), lest your enemy, Satan, will attack and devour you, if he has not already done so (John 10:10). Sin will eventually kill and destroy you, if you do not repent genuinely!

Most drastically, the unpardonable sin, which is a willful rejection of God's gift to Mankind: Jesus Christ remains the unpardonable sin, but the good news is that, you can change that today, by accepting Jesus Christ as your personal Lord and Savior—The choice is yours! God has given you the Free Will, for you to independently decide, whether or not to spend eternity with Him or without Him. I hope you choose wisely and accept Jesus Christ's free gift to you, right now, if you have not already done so genuinely!

Jesus is at the "door" of your heart "knocking," and waiting for you to "let Him in"; have you done so yet? If no, go ahead and let Him into your heart, and it will be the best decision you will ever make.

....

WHAT WAS JESUS' VIEW ON CREATION? DID HE SUPPORT YOUNG OR OLD EARTH?

Question # 22: What was Jesus' View on Creation? Did He Support Young or Old Earth?

Answer: Based on His teachings in the Gospels, Jesus Christ believed in a Young Earth.

The Bible is very clear that God created the heavens and the earth in 6-literal days, and on the 7th day, He "rested" (Genesis chapters 1 and 2). The "rest" here does not imply that God was tired, like we, human beings, experience tiredness. God is Omnipotent and does not experience fatigue. Rather, God rested because He was quite pleased with His creation, and there was nothing else to create; He was essentially done! Thus, He "rested"!

Before I provide a succinct answer to this question, some background is necessary, that way you can perceive the relevance of this question, and why the Lord's view on creation is paramount. There are many critics of the 6-day literal creation, mostly theistic evolutionists, meaning, those who claim to believe in the God of the Bible and in evolution at the same time. Theistic evolutionists are espousing that God used evolution to create the heavens and the earth—this position is unbiblical, to say the least.

The major danger to theistic evolution is that it claims that the earth is millions or even billions of years old. God, in His wisdom, has decided what to share with us and what not to; thus, the exact years of the earth is one of those things that the Bible does not reveal. But God remains the only eye witness to the initial creation of the earth (Job 38:4), as such, we have to take His Word for it, meaning, He created the heavens and the earth in 6-literal days. Nonetheless, based on the timeline of biblical events, Bible scholars have suggested an approximate span of slightly over 6 to 7 thousand years as the age of the earth; and I agree with this position.

If the earth is millions or billions of years old as theistic evolutionists are espousing, then the deaths of creatures had been existing for millions and even billions of years before Adam and Eve were even created. This line of thinking would imply that "Sin" was not the reason for the fall of man as recorded in Genesis chapter 3. So, if sin is not the reason Mankind fell from grace, then Jesus' death was useless, and the entire message of the Gospel is then useless and nullified: you see where this can lead? It is a very dangerous position, in my view.

Much more, to hold to this theistic evolutionists' view, a person would have to literally "tear out" and/or ignore certain key Scriptures from the Bible such as Romans 5:12, which teaches that death entered into the world through sin; and Hebrews 9:22, which teaches that without the shedding of blood, sins cannot be forgiven. Thus, it is impossible, in my view, to argue for theistic evolution from the Scriptures - it is not possible to do so and be honest with the Scriptures at the same time!

Jesus and Creation

Now, let us go back to the original question. With regards to our Lord's view on creation, like already mentioned, I believe that Jesus Christ believed in a young earth. Here is why I say so. In His teaching to the Pharisees (i.e., religious leaders during His time) about marriage (see Mark 10:1-12), the Lord stated, very clearly, that in the beginning, God created them, referring to Adam and Eve, male and female (see Genesis chapters 1 and 2). So let me ask you a question: **When did God create Adam and Eve**? Obviously on the 6th day of creation, right? And not millions or billions of years, right?

Then, in addressing the Pharisees about their hypocrisy and their impending judgment, Jesus' statement shed some insight to help us to understand His view about creation and the timeline of biblical events. The Lord said:

Therefore this generation will be held responsible for the blood of all the prophets that has been shed since the beginning of the world, from the blood of Abel to the blood of Zechariah, who was killed between the altar and the sanctuary. Yes, I tell you, this generation will be held responsible for it all (Luke 11:50-51), (emphasis author's).

Although the Lord was not specifically teaching about creation from the Scripture cited above, His response provides a glimpse of His view on biblical timeline of events. In the Scripture above, the Lord was referring to the first righteous prophet killed in the Old Testament: Abel (see **Genesis chapter 4**), to the last righteous prophet killed during the Old Testament era, Zechariah *(see* **2 Chronicles 24: 20-22),** in accordance with the arrangement of the Hebrew Bible. For those of you unaware, the Hebrew and the English Old Testament books have a slightly different arrangement, although they are the same books. As an example, in the Hebrew Bible, the last book is the book of Chronicles, while in the English Old Testament Bible, the last book is the book of Malachi.

Thus, the Lord's statement in the Scripture above is absolutely significant because, in just a sentence, the Lord provided a solid timeline, from the first to the last prophet killed, as recorded in the Hebrew Bible, thus providing to us a major clue, with regards to the age of the earth. By calculating the number of years in between the murders of Abel to that of Zechariah, the results will only yield thousands of years, and not millions or even billions of years as the theistic evolutionists are purporting.

Much more, Jesus Christ's reference to Satan as a liar from the beginning (John 8:44), is consistent with the Bible account of Mankind's fall from grace (approximately 6 to 7 thousand years ago), as a result of Satan's lies and deception (see Genesis chapter 3). Suffice it to say that, Jesus Christ, God Himself in the flesh, offered to us some major clues that suggest He upheld a younger earth view, consistent with a 6-literal days of creation. Thus, Jesus Christ settled the matter that there is no such thing as "Christian evolution" or "theistic evolutionist", period!

This Jesus Christ, the Creator of the heavens and the earth wants a personal relationship with you. Have you accepted Him as your Lord, Savior, and friend? If no, do that right now, and He will change your destiny for the best.

....

CHAPTER 23

HOW DO I KNOW THAT JESUS REALLY LOVES ME?

Question # 23: How Do I know that Jesus really loves me?

Answer: Because He displayed His Unconditional love for you on the cross, when He died for your sins.

Some of you may laugh at this question. But, as a minister, I have been asked this question countless amount of times. It is indeed a very valid question to ask. You know why? Because in my opinion, love is one of the most abused words in the English language today, and people do not really understand what God's kind of love is all about. As such, they get Agape love (God's kind of love) confused with other types of love, which are primarily emotional.

Briefly, here are the other types of love: (1) Eros , which is romantic type of love, like seen in the movies; (2) Phileo , which is a type of love seen in friendships; and (3) Storge, which is a type of love seen among families members, parents and their children. However, among the different types of love, Agape love remains the type of love with the highest level of stability, satisfaction, and longevity.

Agape love is the only type of love that is not based on your feelings or emotions. It is a type of sacrificial love (i.e., putting others' needs ahead of yours), and it is evident primarily in your actions. Agape love is based on your decision to love someone whether or not the person deserves to be loved, simply because he or she is a human being, created by God.

Much more, agape love is not based on one's appearance, accomplishments, status in society, wealth or possession. It is simply loving someone because he or she is your fellow human being, created in the image of God.

When operating in agape love, you would step out and reach out to others regardless of how you feel. Because agape love is so contrary to all the other types of love which are primarily linked to one's emotions and/or feelings, many individuals become extremely confused when they are told that God loves them. They are often surprised that God would love them, because for the most part, they attempt to gauge God's love for them based on their feelings and/or emotions; because that is how society and the movies have taught people how to receive and express love — which is a stark contrast to how God loves us.

He Loves You Unconditionally

God's kind of love is 100% unconditional (i.e., Agape love). God is love in His very nature. And the apex of His love was displayed on the Cross, when God Himself, in the person of Jesus Christ died on the cross for the sins of the entire world, thus paving the way for anyone who so desires, to have a relationship with Him. For the Bible tells us that: *"For this is how God loved the world: He gave his one and only Son, so that everyone who believes in him will not perish but have eternal life"* (John 3:16; New Living Translation), (emphasis author's).

God does not give love, nor does He decide whether or not to love —He is love in His nature and being. So whether or not you accept this Truth, God loves you unconditionally. By unconditionally, I am referring to the fact that God loves you as you are, right now, regardless of how you view yourself, and He wants you to come to Him, so that He can change you to become the person He created you to be. Here is a classic example of other attributes of God's kind of love:

Love is patient and kind. Love is not jealous or boastful or proud or rude. It does not demand its own way. It is not irritable, and it keeps no record of being wronged. It does not rejoice about injustice but rejoices whenever the truth wins out. Love never gives up, never loses faith, is always hopeful,

and endures through every circumstance. (1 Corinthians 13:4-
7; New Living Translation), (emphasis author's).

> **In spite of all of the wrongs you have
> committed against Jesus, He still loves you,
> because His nature is love. Jesus Christ will never
> condone sin, nor ignore disobedience. But He
> wants to forgive you, and cleanse you from all
> of your sins, thereby giving you a new start in
> life. Remember, Jesus hates the sin, but loves the
> sinner, so ask Him to help you to change into the
> person he created you to be.**

Many people get God's loving nature confused with
His justice.

> **They often wonder, if God loves us, why would
> He punish or send people to hell? Firstly, like I
> have already explained in the preceding chapters,
> God does not send anyone to hell; rather, He
> has provided a way for people not to go to hell,
> but people, by their own choosing, go to hell.
> Secondly, God is just and fair; He hates sin, which
> means in His love, He still has to carry out justice
> and punishment.**

Many people want to hear all about God's character of love, but they do not want to hear about His justice; it cannot be that way. For love to be in its fullest operation, justice must be carried out, and since God is 100% perfectly holy and righteous, in His justice, sin has to be punished. And unfortunately, many Christians often attribute their pain and suffering to the fact that God is punishing them somehow. Yet, the Bible is very clear that there is no guilt and condemnation for a true follower of the Lord Jesus (Romans 8:1-2).

On the contrary, many people have made wrong decisions, which have opened the door for the enemy, Satan, to attack them (John 10:10), and they are blaming God. Satan is not stronger than God. But because of disobedience to God, many people have limited His presence and protective power in their lives; and as such, that has given Satan direct access into their lives, and he is "wreaking havoc", killing and destroying them, which is his primary goal (John 10:10).

God has given each of us a Free Will (see Genesis chapters 1 through 3), thus people continuously abuse their Free Will , leading to the much pain and suffering we are experiencing in the world today. It is again because of God's love, that He did not create human beings as "Robots" that He could control and manipulate at His whim. Rather, because of His love, He has given each of us a Free Will, so that those who desire can freely love Him back, voluntarily. But we have an enemy called Satan, who is continuously deceiving people, leading them to abuse their Free Will, and thus causing them to question God's love for them; these people are then turning around and blaming God, and questioning His love for them. Do not be deceived — God indeed loves you, unconditionally.

So, yes, God loves you, regardless of how you feel; and do not rely on your emotions to evaluate God's love for you. The Bible teaches us that as Christians, we should live out our Christian journey by faith, and not by how we feel (2 Corinthians 5:7). Hence, to start experiencing the love of God, I recommend that you meditate on Scriptures that teach that God is love, and that He loves you.

For example, study the entire epistles of 1st, 2nd, and 3rd John over and over. Meditate, meaning, pause, and ponder on these Truths about God's love to you, over a prolonged period of time, and as you do that, it will become rooted in your soul and become your reality. I heard a true story about a lady who was severely struggling with depression, fear, and discouragement. Her Pastor recommended that she should study the three epistles of John over a period of time until the Scriptures of God's love speak to her heart. Well, this lady took up the challenge, and for about 6 months, she only studied and meditated on 1st, 2nd, and 3rd John. Thereafter, her life was transformed 180 degrees, and all of her emotional issues disappeared effortlessly, and she came off of her medications. This is a powerful testimony of how the revelation of the love of God is a potent antidote against emotional instability. Hence, I recommend that you likewise meditate on God's love for you.

As you meditate on God's love, while asking the Holy Spirit to help you to comprehend this Truth, you will start to get a deeper revelation of how much God loves you. Once you come to this firm Truth about God's love for you, it will become easier for you to express agape love to others; because, before you can reach out to others in agape love, you must first have experienced it yourself. Much more, once you are "grounded" with the Truth of God's love for you, Satan will not be able to tempt you to question God's love for you. Yes indeed, Jesus Christ, God Himself, loves you, unconditionally.

Do you have a personal relationship with this Jesus Christ who loves you unconditionally? If the answer is no, I recommend that you ask Him to come into your life right now, and you will begin to experience His unfathomable love for you right at this moment!!

....

WAS JESUS CHRIST BORN AGAIN?

Question # 24: Was Jesus Christ Born Again?

Answer: Absolutely Not: He was not born again! He did not have to be.

To answer this question succinctly, a brief background is necessary about what "born again" really means. In an encounter with a religious leader called Nicodemus, out of the Gospel of John chapter 3, our Lord Jesus said that except a person is born again, he or she cannot enter into God's Kingdom, meaning, have a relationship with the Only True living God of the heavens and the earth (vv.1-3), the God of the Bible. Although I have explained the concept of born again in previous chapters, I want to refresh your memory here as well. Remember that human beings are born into this world as sinners, because we all inherit a Sinful Nature from our common ancestors: Adam and Eve, who fell from grace after they transgressed God's law; I hope you recall?

And, I already explained how every human being experiences a physical birth (i.e., to be birthed into this world physically by your mother). But in order to have a relationship with God (i.e., to be reconciled with God), a spiritual birth is essential (i.e., you have to be born again); I hope you recall this as well? Hence, only those who have inherited a Sinful Nature, such as all human beings, require this spiritual birth called "born again", so that their sins might be forgiven by God.

He Was/Is Divine

With the above explanation in the forefront, remember that Jesus Christ did not experience a physical birth like every other human being in the history of the world has experienced or will ever experience. Jesus Christ experienced a divine birth. As explained already, Jesus Christ, God Himself in the flesh, was the Word (i.e., Word of God) that was made flesh (i.e., became flesh and bones, meaning, He became a human being) (John 1:1-14). Christ Jesus came into this world in a supernaturally divine manner — His mother, Mary, was supernaturally pregnant by the Holy Spirit. As such, the Lord Jesus had no earthly Father; He therefore did not inherit a Sinful Nature because the supernatural conception by His mother prevented Him from being contaminated by sin and/or the Sinful Nature of Mankind.

Only "fallen" human beings, like every human being in the history of the human race, with an inherited Sinful Nature, need a spiritual birth, and

**thus, reconciliation with God through the born
again birth, in order for their sins to be forgiven.
Thus, Jesus Christ, Who was God Himself in the
flesh, Who took upon a human body, was born
divine into this world, and lived a sinless life; and
as such, required no reconciliation with God, nor
needed to be born again.**

So absolutely NOT: Jesus Christ was not born again —
He was God Himself! The Bible teaches that Jesus Christ took
the sins of the entire world upon His sinless body, in order for
each one of us to become born again; that way, we could have a
relationship with God the Father, if we so desire (2 Corinthians
5:21). There is Only One name given unto man by which true
salvation must come, the name Jesus Christ (Acts 4:12). Jesus
Christ is The Only source of eternal life (John 6:47-48), and
your Only Way to The Only True God of the Universe (John
14:6).

Do you know this Jesus Christ who died for you? If
Yes, great! If No, you can invite Him into your life right now!
He is waiting for you, and He is eager for you to ask Him into
your life, today (Revelation 3:20); will you do that, right now?
It will be the best decision you ever made; and you will never
regret it, guaranteed!

....

IS IT RELEVANT TO PRAY IN THE NAME OF JESUS?

Question # 25: Is it Relevant to Pray in the Name of Jesus?

Answer: Yes, it is relevant to pray in the name of Jesus, because we can only approach God through the merit of Jesus' redemptive work on the cross.

Before I answer this question, I want to first establish a few things about prayer. In its simplistic definition, prayer simply means communication with God, like you would talk with a friend. For the Christian, the primary purpose for prayer is for God's will to manifest on the earth, and in our respective lives. It is God's will for us, His children, to present our requests to Him through the channel of prayer (Matthew 6:5-13). But, the Bible teaches that our prayers should be uttered in the name of Jesus Christ, Whose righteousness we have inherited at the time of our salvation. Thus, we should pray in the name of Jesus because:

1. Firstly, there is power and authority in the name of Jesus (Matthew 28:18; John 17:1-2). **As Christians, we have been given, by Jesus Himself, delegated power and authority to ask anything, in His name, to the extent that whatever we are asking is within the confines of God's Word.** So when we pray, we are relying on the power and authority in His name, because on our own, we are useless to accomplish anything (John 15:5); but with Jesus on our side, we can accomplish anything in accordance with God's will.

2. Secondly, the Lord Himself teaches that we should approach God in His name; and in doing that, we will glorify God the Father (John 14:13-14; 16:24). Thus, when we pray in the name of Jesus, it means that we are asking as His representatives, here on the earth. **This is crucial because when we pray, we are, in essence, asking for the will of Jesus Christ, our Lord, Savior and Mediator, to manifest on the earth, and in our individual lives, so that God the Father will be glorified.** Even though as Christians, we are joint heirs with Christ Jesus (i.e., whatever belongs to the Lord Jesus belongs to us, in God's Kingdom), we still cannot approach God on our own merit. We must only approach God through Christ, because of our relationship with Him. <u>Therefore, when we approach God in the name of Jesus, we are surrendering our own will, thereby depending and trusting on the will of Jesus to manifest.</u>

3. Thirdly, by praying in the name of Jesus, we are believing, by faith, that God will hear us, because we are 100% depending on the merit of Jesus Christ, who has enabled us to have good moral and spiritual standing in front of God the Father. In essence, Jesus is our mediator before God the Father; and because we have placed our faith in Him, we are trusting that God will answer our prayers because of our faith and hope in Jesus Christ.

4. Fourthly, we pray in the name of Jesus in order to accomplish God's will on the earth as fruit bearing Christians. The Lord teaches that when we abide in Him (i.e., stay 100% focused on Him), and practice His Word (i.e., His teachings as found in the Bible), we can ask God the Father for anything in His name, and He will give it to us; that way, we can bear much fruit for God's Kingdom (i.e., bring many to God's Kingdom and help them to grow, etc), which will be an excellent evidence that we are His true followers (John 15: 1-8).

It Is Not A "Magic Formula"

It is important to note that praying in the name of Jesus in and of itself is not the "magic formula" for your prayers to be answered.

Firstly, you must have genuine faith in His name, in order to call upon His name in prayer and expect results. Secondly, if what you are praying for does not glorify God, and/or is outside of His will as expressed in the Bible, then your prayer in the name of Jesus will yield no results. Thirdly, the motives behind your prayer is a major determinant whether or not your prayers are answered.

For those of you interested in an in-depth study about the topic of prayer, I recommend that you get my book titled: **Are you Moving Forward with Jesus? How to Excel in Your Identity in Christ.** In that book, the longest chapter, almost 50 pages, is dedicated to the topic of prayer. So check the resource list at the end of this book on how to obtain that book.

The Bible is very clear, that we are only to pray in the name of Jesus. Thus praying in the name of Mary, who is the beloved mother of our Lord Jesus, is unbiblical. And, it is also unbiblical to pray in the name of various so-called "saints", like some people do today. Praying in any other name besides the name of Jesus Christ is one of the reasons for many unanswered prayers today, **because there is power and authority in only One name: the name of Jesus Christ!**

I want to conclude this section by adding that, when it is all "said and done", God deals with us at a heart level. Thus, if a genuine believer prays and forgets and/or misses to end the prayer in the name of Jesus, it is my belief that God still answers such prayers, because God knows our hearts — He is after the sincerity and motives behind our prayers. Besides, our personal Advocate, Teacher and Counselor, the Holy Spirit, even intercedes for us in prayer, when we are unable to pray (Romans 8:26-27). So, there is always hope for us, God's beloved children, even when we miss to pray in the name of Jesus.

So, now that you know the relevance of praying in the name of Jesus, next time you pray, ask yourself if whatever you are asking God for is what your Lord and Savior, Jesus Christ, would have prayed about to God the Father. If Yes, then proceed to pray in faith; and if No, then do not pray, period!

If we, as Christians, can put this simple practice to use during our prayer time, I believe, we will avoid a lot of the heartache that comes along when we pray outside of God's will and expect Him to answer.

So, have you prayed for God to forgive you of All of your sins? And have you accepted His forgiveness through Jesus Christ? If no, proceed and do that today and God will answer your prayer, and Jesus will come and dwell in your heart by faith, and your life will never be the same!

....

WHAT'S NEXT?

I started this project with the goal of providing very basic, straight forward, to the point answers to 25 of the toughest questions about the real Jesus Christ of the true Christian Bible. And I believe I have done so in a manner that will be easy for you, the reader, to come to a true biblical knowledge and understanding of your personal Lord and Savior, Jesus Christ. While I could easily have addressed over a 100 such questions, it is my belief that, the answers to these 25 questions I have provided in this book will provide you with a solid foundation for you to build on.

It is also my hope that, with this solid foundation, you will become well equipped to educate others about the hypostatic nature of Jesus Christ as 100% human being, and 100% God. This is crucial because the hypostatic nature of Jesus Christ is the primary reason that many cults, such as the Jehovah's Witnesses and the Mormons, and all other world man-made religions are misled, and as such, are continuing with their heretical teachings about Christ.

And, if you are already a true follower of Christ, I hope that this book has strengthened and emboldened you to want to step out in faith, and to share your faith with others. Much more, I hope that you can now, with much confidence, correctly teach and/or educate others, about the true Jesus Christ that you serve!

And if you are not a follower of Christ, I hope that I have provided answers to some of your questions, to the extent that you are now open, and willing to ask Jesus Christ into your life. I guarantee you, if you genuinely become a follower of Jesus Christ, He will absolutely change your life beyond what you can imagine!

He Changed My Life

I am a living testimony that Jesus Christ will profoundly change your life. Besides healing me of metastasis colon cancer, and a host of other diseases in 2009 (I have discussed my testimony in another book, check the resource list at the end of this book on how to obtain that book, if you are interested), my relationship with God through Jesus Christ, and the empowering of the Holy Spirit has transformed my life. Today, I am enjoying supernatural peace, contentment and joy in my life, that no amount of money, career success, status, or earthly relationships can provide or even come close to providing.

The many worldly things that many people attribute or associate with true joy and peace can never satisfy your soul's deepest desire to know your Creator, the God of the Bible. I make this statement with much confidence because I had the earthly/worldly things that many people believe will bring peace, but "those things" did not, in my case, and I believe it is the same in the case of countless others. For example, academically, I excelled, and I am the recipient of many highly acclaimed academic awards.

Academically, I attained my goals of publication, by publishing "top notch" research and review papers that are still making major contributions in advancement of knowledge in the academic realm and clinically. I worked as a model for over 12 years, had my own TV show, and could have dated any gentleman I wanted to; and I indeed dated a lot of so called "outwardly successful men", but guess what? I was never happy, much less experienced the peace and true joy I was searching for. You know why? Because happiness is solely based on what is happening to you, which means it fluctuates, depending on the day. What I needed was a heartfelt relationship with Jesus Christ, and His joy and peace which are constant.

And, as a minister and a doctor, I have counseled dozens of millionaires and others whom according to worldly standards, would be considered successful; yet, these individuals are the most miserable and emotionally distraught individuals I have met. Besides, all you have to do is look at Hollywood, and it will become obvious that wealth, appearances, achievements, etc, cannot provide any true joy, peace and meaning in our lives.

Because, if it did, many millionaires and so called celebrities in Hollywood and elsewhere would not be depending on illicit drugs and other prescriptive drugs to manage their emotions. And the sad thing is that, all these external substances such as drugs, sex, etc, cannot cure the "root" of the problem.

Only Jesus Christ is The answer to the darkness in man's heart.

So happiness is not what you want; rather, you want true joy, which only comes from a personal relationship with God through Christ.

In my situation, just like many others, in spite of my "worldly" success, I never experienced true joy, peace, contentment, meaning and purpose in life until I totally rededicated my life to Jesus Christ over 14 years ago. Keep in mind that I said, rededicated! Because, even though I was a Christian, and have been one from a young girl, even before I was 10 years old; I knew the Lord, but I was not "walking" with Him— there is a big difference between the two conditions!

Many Christians have accepted Jesus Christ as their personal Lord and Savior, but they remain carnal; that is to say, they are still living their lives as unbelievers, making decisions based on their five senses, rather than the precepts from the Bible; and as such, they are miserable, much like I was. Yet, the Bible admonishes us to live and walk by faith, rather than by our emotions and/or what we can perceive out of our senses or from the environment.

Now that I am "walking" daily with God, I am experiencing the blessed life He created me to enjoy, and I regret why I did not rededicate my life to the Lord sooner! As I look back in my life, I could have prevented a lot of the pain, suffering and heartache that I experienced, because of carnality.

Jesus Is The Only Answer

How I wish I could convince you to rededicate your life to the Lord now, right now, if you are a Christian who is not totally committed to Him! And how I wish I could enable you to see, if you are an unbeliever, how much you are wasting your life right now, if Jesus is not your Lord and Savior. Because, apart from personally knowing and "walking" daily with the True living God of the Bible through a relationship with His Only Son Jesus Christ, and the enabling of the Holy Spirit, life is useless.

True Christianity answers the three major questions about life: (1) who you are, referring to your identity; (2) why you are here on the earth, referring to your divine purpose; and (3) what happens to you after you die, referring to your eternity. Jesus Christ is the Only person in the history of the world, who has the answers to these three of life's fundamental questions!

Don't you want to personally have these three questions answered? God, who created you, has placed eternity in your heart (Ecclesiastes 3:11). Thus, I am convinced that you want to have these questions answered —every human being alive does!

Accept to Follow Jesus Christ Now

Over 2000 years ago, Jesus Christ asked His disciples this questions: **"Who do people say the Son of Man is?"** (Matthew 16:13), emphasis author's. Today, I am asking you the same question: Who do you say Jesus Christ is? Hopefully, you have come into agreement with who Jesus Christ says He is! Because, unfortunately, He has only given us two choices: Accept or reject Him, period!

And unfortunately, your opinion of Jesus Christ does not change who He is; in essence, your opinion is irrelevant to the absolute Truth that He is God 100% and man 100%. You must make a decision, for or against Him, and deal with the consequences of your decision in this life, and in all eternity. And keep in mind that by not making a decision, you are choosing to deny Him.

As I have been saying throughout this book, Only Jesus Christ has The ticket to eternity with God. As already described, no other human being can show you the way, except Jesus Christ. He has already paved the way for you to have direct access to God the Father; the ticket has been paid for, so why would you want to reject the FREE ticket and end up in hell? You now know the Truth—and it is your decision to choose wisely. God has given you a Free Will, and I pray that you will use your Free Will wisely, to make the best decision ever: inviting Jesus Christ into your life.

Do not postpone this decision, because tomorrow is not guaranteed. You could die tonight. I do not want to scare you, but people die in their sleep every day. You want to be 100% certain about what will happen to you the moment you die. Death will come, it is the all time equalizer; all of us will die, someday. But, do you know where you are going after you take your last breath here on this earth? Be certain today. If you are ready to accept Jesus Christ into your life, and you have been reading this book thus far, you know exactly what to do, so do it, right now. But if you need help doing so, simply say the prayer below:

Dear God, I ask You to forgive me for all of my sins. I believe in my heart that Jesus Christ was, and is God in the flesh, Who died for my personal sins, and You raised Him from the dead on the third day. Forgive me for not acknowledging this Truth before. Right now, I accept Your forgiveness, and I am asking You, Jesus Christ, to come into my life as my personal Lord and Savior. I denounce all other false gods in my life, and I have chosen You as my God. I ask that You fill me with Your Holy

Spirit, God, so that I can live as a Christian to glorify You. By faith, I receive Your forgiveness of my sins, and I declare, today, that I am a true Christian, in Jesus name, AMEN

If you said that prayer genuinely, based on the authority of God's Word, The Only inspired and infallible Holy Scripture, I declare you are a true Christian. You may or may not have experienced an emotional feeling after saying that prayer; it is okay, because as Christians, we live by faith as stated in God's Word, and not by how we feel (2 Corinthians 5:7). So if you were sincere when you said that prayer, take it by faith that God has accepted you. Welcome into God's Kingdom. You have now been sealed with the Holy Spirit, and your eternity is secured (Ephesians 1:13). Feel free to contact us so we can send you more resources to help you grow as a child of God.

....

CONCLUDING REMARKS

After reading this book thus far, I hope you are in agreement that Jesus Christ is your only hope in this life and in eternity. Hence, if you have not already accepted Jesus Christ as your personal Lord and Savior, this is the right time to do so before you close this book; hopefully, you will do so in faith.

Thereafter, the immediate next step after you have accepted Jesus Christ into your life is to get a copy of the Holy Bible. Any modern translation, such as the New International Version (NIV), New King James Version (NKJV), New Living Translation (NLT), etc, will be appropriate. **But, do not get the Jehovah's Witnesses Bible called New World Translation (NWT), or the Mormons Scripture called the Book of Mormons, because these are grossly falsified scriptures, for reasons already described in this book.**

Once you get a Bible, start reading it, beginning with the Gospel of John, then to the epistles of 1st, 2nd, and 3rd John. These few books of the Bible will teach you further about who Jesus Christ is, and His unconditional love for you.

Thereafter, go to the Old Testament and begin your study with the book of Genesis.

I also recommend that you contact our ministry and sign up to get our in-depth audio Podcast, which focuses on teaching across the entire Bible, from the book of Genesis to the book of Revelation, if you are interested in studying through the entire Bible. This Podcast will transform your life, as you will be taught the Word of God, and also, you will be able to listen to it, at your convenience.

Next, find a local Bible believing and practicing church and start attending. Be certain that the church you choose to attend uses the Bible as their primary authority, and has evidence of biblical principles operating in their church. As you become rooted in a local church, get involved in ministry there, and begin fellowshipping with other believers, and grow in your faith.

Congratulations to you! You are now a beloved child of God!

BIBLIOGRAPHY

Bibliography

American Psychiatric Association. Diagnostic And Statistical Manual of Mental Disorders, 5th edition (DSM-5™). American Psychiatric Publishing, Washington DC, 2013.

Bruce L Shelley. Church History in Plain Language (4th edition). Nashville: Nelson, 2008.

Cruse, C. F. Eusebius': Ecclesiastical History. Complete and Unabridged (New Updated Edition). Peabody, MA: Hendrickson Publishers, 1998.

J. D. Douglas & Merrill C. Tenney (editors). NIV Compact Dictionary of the Bible. Grand Rapids: Zondervan, 1989.

Josh McDowell and Bill Wilson. Evidence for the Historical Jesus: A Compelling Case for His Life and His Claims. Oregon: Harvest House Publishers, 1988.

Josh McDowel and Sean McDowel. Evidence for the Resurrection: What It Means For Your Relationship with God. California: Regal, 1996.

Sproul, R. C. Defending Your Faith: An Introduction to Apologetics. Crossway, 2003.

Stoner, P.W. & Newman, R. C. Science Speaks. Moody

Publishers, 1958.

Walvoord, J. F. Every Prophecy Of the Bible. Colorado Springs, CO: David Cook, 2011.

www.icr.org.

www.jw.org.

www.mormon.org.

W. E. Vine, Merrill F. Unger, William White, Jr. Vine's Complete Expository Dictionary of Old and New Testament Words. Nashville: Nelson, 1996.

Whiston W. The Works of Josephus: Complete and Unabridged (New Updated Edition). Peabody, MA: Hendrickson Publishers, 1987.

Zacharias, R and Geisler, Norman (General Editors). Who Made God? And Answers to Over 100 Other Tough Questions of Faith. Zondervan, 2003.

OTHER BOOKS BY DR TANYI

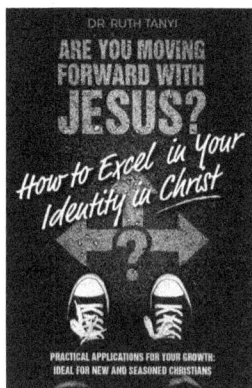

Are You Moving Forward with Jesus? How to Excel In Your Identity in Christ

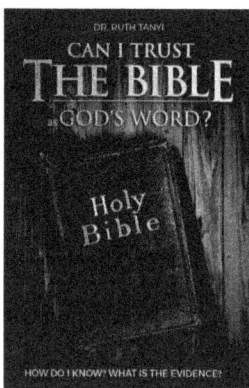

Can I Trust the Bible as God's Word? How do I know? What is the Evidence?

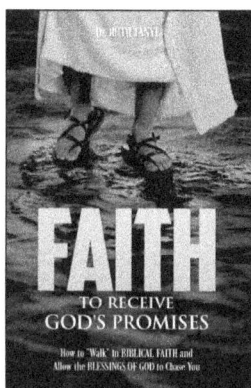

Faith to Receive God's Promises. How to "Walk" in Biblical Faith and Allow the Blessings of God to Chase You

---
COMING SOON!

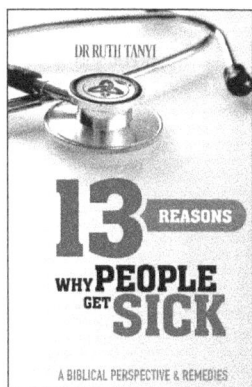

13 Reasons why People Get Sick! A Biblical Perspective & Remedies

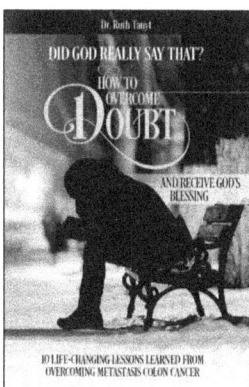

Did God Really Say that? How to Overcome Doubt and Receive God's Promises: 10 Life-Changing Lessons Learned from Overcoming Metastasis Colon Cancer.

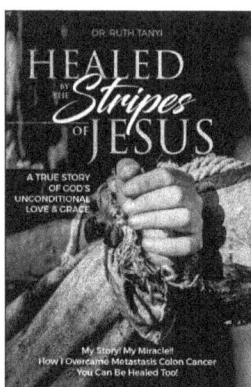

Healed by the Stripes of Jesus: A True Story of God's Unconditional Grace and Love: My Story! My Miracle! How I Overcame Metastasis Colon Cancer: You can Be Healed Too!

AUDIO CD TEACHING LIBRARY

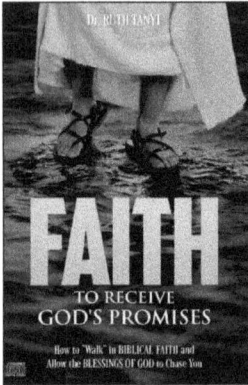

Faith to Receive God's Promises: How to "Walk" in Biblical Faith and Allow the Blessings of God to Chase You

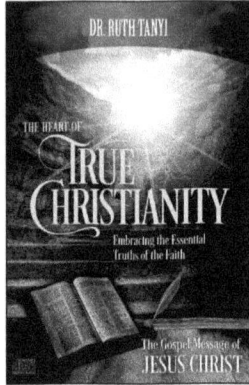

The Heart of True Christianity: The Gospel Message of Jesus Christ: Answers to 10 Major Questions Pertaining to Your Salvation in Christ Jesus

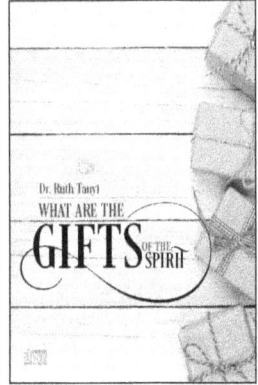

What Are the Gifts of the Spirit?

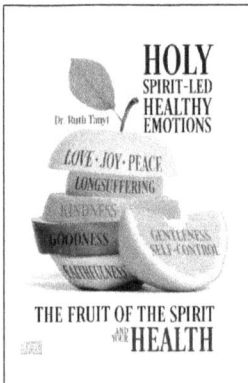

Holy Spirit-Led Healthy Emotions: The Fruit of the Spirit and Your Health

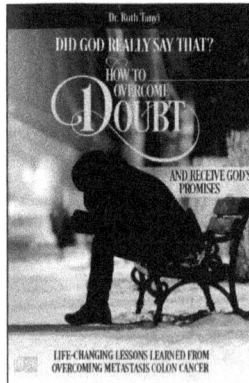

How to Overcome Doubt and Receive God's Promises

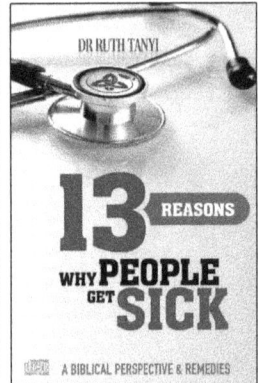

13 Reasons Why People Get Sick: A Biblical Perspective & Remedies

AUDIO CD TEACHING LIBRARY

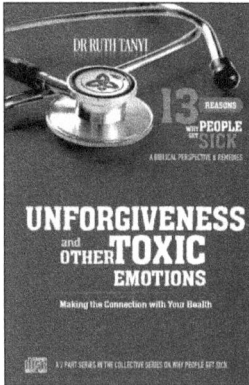

Unforgiveness and Other Toxic Emotions: How to Walk in Forgiveness

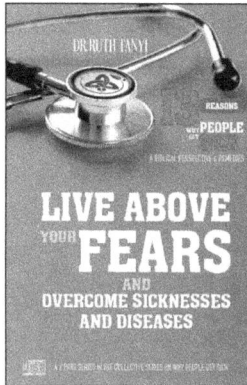

Live Above Your Fears & Overcome Sicknesses and Diseases

Be Anxious No More

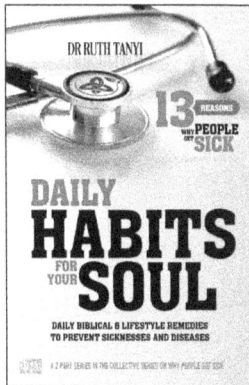

Daily Habits For Your Soul

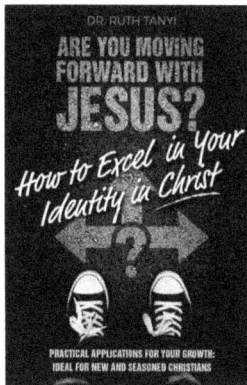

Are You Moving Forward with Jesus? How to Excel In Your Identity in Christ

OTHER TEACHINGS BY DR TANYI

Discipleship Bible Teaching Series

Biblical Preventive Health with Dr Ruth ® Magazine

13 Reasons Why True Christianity is Different: A Wall Mount Poster
A Call to Action Poster

Visit **Dr Ruth Tanyi Ministries YouTube Channel** and watch our FREE Devotional Teachings, Plus Other FREE Teachings at your convenience, 24/7. Subscribe to our YouTube Channel and start enjoying our Free Teachings Today.

Visit www.Drruthtanyi.org/blog and watch our FREE Devotional Teachings.

Obtaining Ministry Resources

To get more information about the above ministry resources, please visit our Website: **www.DrRuthTanyi.org**

Contact Information
You Can also Email or Contact us:

Dr Ruth Tanyi Ministries, Inc
P O BOX 1806
Loma Linda, CA, 92354, USA
Email: Info@DrRuthtanyi.org

ABOUT THE AUTHOR

Dr. Ruth Tanyi, DrPH, NP, ACSM HFS; CNS; MA Ministry

Dr. Ruth Tanyi is a Bible Teacher, Doctor of Preventive Care/Integrative Medicine, Board Certified Nutritionist and Exercise Physiologist. She is the founder /CEO of Dr. Ruth Tanyi Ministries, a non-denominational Christian, non-profit ministry located in San Bernardino, California, with primary focus on spreading the uncompromising Gospel of Jesus Christ; sharing God's unconditional love and grace, while concurrently teaching others how to integrate Bible-based principles with medical lifestyle practices in order to prevent and overcome diseases.

Even before being healed by God from metastasis colon cancer and other diseases in 2009, Dr Ruth felt called by God into ministry. However, since her healing and experiential knowledge and revelation of the love and grace of God, she has become an ardent student and teacher of the Word of God.

Dr Ruth's greatest desire is to tell others about God's unconditional love and grace, which she supernaturally experienced, and to teach individuals the lessons she learnt from God on how she received her healing, thereby helping others to be set free as well. Since God is no respecter of persons, Dr Ruth wants to strengthen others by reminding them that if God can heal her, He (God), can set them free as well regardless of the doctor's diagnosis or prognosis: All things are possible with God.

Dr Ruth is a public speaker and author, and offers a CD and DVD teaching library in addition to books on various topics ranging from the essential doctrines of true Christianity, to teachings on the very essential connection between God's Word and Medicine. Dr Ruth is also actively involved in the Body of Christ via her involvement with other ministries in advancing the Gospel of Jesus Christ, and in espousing the necessity of knowing God's Word. She considers herself to be a non-denominational Bible believing Christian, with a deep desire to fellowship and work with fellow brothers and sisters in Christ, regardless of denominational differences, for the common goal of advancing God's Kingdom and proclaiming the Gospel Message of Jesus Christ in these last days.

Prior to her calling into ministry, she had produced numerous TV series on lifestyle practices and disease prevention which aired throughout Southern California, and are still broadcasting through various media such as True Health Broadcasting Network, and SmartLifestyleTV, a division of LLBN Network worldwide. Her award winning TV series "Bad Sugar"® which focused on Diabetes, in addition to her other TV teachings on lifestyle and disease prevention continues to change thousands of lives.

Dr Tanyi has published numerous academic peer-reviewed journal articles and research papers, and she continues to serve as external reviewer for various International academic peer-reviewed journals. She is still pursuing her academic research in the area of lifestyle practices in preventing and overcoming depression. She has been nominated and selected in WHO IS WHO IN AMERICA and in WHO IS WHO IN Medicine and Healthcare. She is in private practice in San Bernardino California, and lives in Southern California.

For more information visit www.DrRuthTanyi.org, or to contact Dr Tanyi to speak at your event, church or non-Christian event, email her at: DrRuth@DrRuthTanyi.org, or call (909) 383 7978.

www.ingramcontent.com/pod-product-compliance
Lightning Source LLC
Chambersburg PA
CBHW021230090426
42740CB00006B/464